IN MY FATHER'S IMAGE

Poems, pictures, and messages for the seasons of life

David C. Bosley

All scriptures are from the KJV of the Bible.

Cover Photography by Tim Bosley

In My Father's Image
Written by
David C. Bosley

www.dayspringministries.org

dayspringchurch@att.net

ISBN 9780692308653

Library of Congress 2014918685

Dayspring Touch Press
2127 Doctor's Park Drive
Columbus, IN 47203

Amid the flow of what often is a complex life for us all, Pastor David C. Bosley shares with us his seasoned thoughts on a number of meditations. It is the true privilege of the reader to reflect along with the author on such timeless meditations as God, and family. The sweet influences of unique poetry and numerous gems of wisdom that lift us in our daily lives are truly rare. Congratulations!

Bishop H. Anthony Stephens M.TH. D.D.
Jurisdictional Bishop
Higher Ground Always Abounding Assemblies, Inc.

David Bosley is a man who loves God, who loves his family, and who loves others. He is a large, yet gentle man. His voice can be big and booming but his touch can be gentle and soothing. "In My Father's Image" is much more than metrical rhythms and rhyming words. It is an expression of life viewed through the eyes of the author who sees beyond the surface and searches the soul. His writings will make you smile, think, question, and hopefully even respond.

Mark Teike, Pastor M. Div
St. Peter's Lutheran Church
719 Fifth Street
Columbus, IN 47201

In My Father's Image is an inspirational and encouraging collection of poems beautifully written for the ear to hear, the mouth to share and the heart to love. The name itself is one that gives a sense of knowing that God is talking through one of His as he puts pen to paper. These poems can move us from a season of pain in our lives to one of pure joy. It would serve us all to walk and talk with these writings on our lips, In My Father's Image.

Paulette Roberts
Educator
Founder & Director
Columbus Enrichment Program

When David let me know he planned to pen a book on his poems, I immediately knew it would be an insightful and intense book. Couple the insight and intensity of the book with the myriad of situations he has dealt with and you have recipes for a multi-volume project. I've listened to his poems over the years and realize you don't get the majority of the content until you have had a chance to review and reflect. Sure you get the jest of the poem as its spoken, and the context during the reading; but the meat lies below the surface and takes some work to digest. I can appreciate the time he has spent in making the poems. His poems are a **Sudoku** *of sorts from life experiences. Get this book!*

Timothy T. Bosley
Controls Engineer
Cummins Inc

Dedication

I dedicate this book to my mother. While Dad worked two and sometimes three jobs she raised my brothers and sisters to love to read and to appreciate the power of words. I dedicate it to her for all she gave me, and all she taught me. I dedicate it to her for making words important to me, and for buying me a book whenever I was good. Thank you, Momma for making the Word of God and a relationship with Jesus Christ important to me. She was a queen before her time.

STAY THERE

"Men may fail you, days may change, heaven and earth may pass away. But the foundation of His WORD will not decay."

Stay There, Stay There.
Stay right there. Stay in the WORD.
When the Devil tries to tempt you, and your strength begins to fail.
When your steps are tried and unsure, you must leave the beaten trail.
There is one who feeds the birds, so you know he'll answer you.
If you stay there in the WORD. His power will bring you through.
When you face the hardest test, And you think you'll surely fall,
Just give your very best. You can answer to His call.
For your Masters voice you've heard,
If you stay there in His WORD.

Leotha V. Bosley © 1/22/93

Special Thanks and Acknowledgments

While I have been inspired to write the poems as they came, this book was not a singular effort. I would like to thank all of those that helped me along the way. Special thanks goes to:

- My lovely wife, Charlene "Candy Girl" Bosley. For your love and inspiration.
- My darling daughter, Christen Bosley. For recording and mix assistance.
- Clyde Flemmings, one of my brothers. For your prayers.
- Joseph M. Bosley, one of my brothers. For your encouraging words.
- Thomas Bosley, one of my brothers. For your design assistance.
- Francis Bosley, Tommy's wife. For editorial insights.
- Brooke and Blaire Bosley, Tommy's oldest daughters, For your additional design and editorial work.
- Tim Bosley, one of my brothers. For your editorial assistance and inspirational words.
- Kay Bosley, Tim's wife. For your editorial assistance and cover layout insights.
- Pat Evans, one of my sisters. For your editorial insights and suggestions.
- Kat Hankins, one of my sisters. For your prayers and encouragement.
- Sam Bosley, yet another brother. For your mastering work on the Bonus CD, for Dimecshion Multimedia: dimencshion@gmail.com
- Donel Sallard, for your musical insight and work on my songs: In The Beginning, & I Want To See Jesus.

- Shannon Luckey, for your exquisite bass rifts on The Rapture.
- James Wood, Sr. and his son Jerome Wood, for your masterful praise song collaboration, "In The Beginning".
- Sue Breeding, for your training and priceless insight.
- Dayspring Church Family, for blessing your Pastor.

Foreword

Obviously the title of this collection of modern day poems "In My Father's Image" authored by the very skilled, gifted, anointed, and intellectual David C. Bosley, reflects a tremendous admiration and love for both his earthly father, and his Heavenly Father. This is very significant because of the positive influence that his natural father has had on him by being an excellent role model for he and his siblings, and of course the life transforming power that he attests to that his Heavenly Father has had on him has enabled him to be all that he is today.

David also speaks to us in commanding poetic tones of the tremendous impact that his caring and loving mother has had on him in helping to shape him to be the individual he is today.

He is also successful in telling in just a few words with a poetic flare the story of how that two different men, one in the United States of American, and the other one in South Africa, each struggled and sacrificed greatly to help liberate their nation from the tyranny of injustice and the oppression of a people simply because of the color of their skin.

David also redirects our attention to the eternal sphere, by sharing with us and perhaps introducing to some a Biblical concept called "The Rapture of the Church." He tells us that we must be ready for the Rapture.

It is my belief that you can be greatly enriched both naturally and spiritually by reading this wonderful and moving collection of poems authored by our good friend and brother in Christ, Dr. David C. Bosley.

Dr. Charles A. Sims, D. Min.
Diocesan Bishop
4th Episcopal District
Pentecostal Assemblies of The World, Inc.

Contents

Introduction

Folk have always told me that I look like my Dad. I cannot argue. I do believe that I have brothers that look more like him than I. Never-the-less, I have heard it said more than once, "The Bosley's have some strong genes!" This is one of the reasons I was inspired to pen the title, **In My Father's Image**. In fact I like to say, the Lord gave me the title.

The play on, **In My Father's Image** does not stop there. You should value that in addition to my earthly father, I recognize a heavenly Father. In this vein I believe that the words of the Bible are true and as such, I believe that we have all been created in God's image. He is also the Father that I reference. So you can then appreciate that this is also a strong basis for the title.

You should also understand that each of the chapter headings incorporate a word that roughly translates as **image**. So in this way I have been further moved to make each chapter a reflection of the whole. The chapter headings follow the title flow in this vein: picture, representation, icon, figure, likeness, illustration, reflection, copy, look, appearance, vision, idea, view, aura, and impression. In other words they are all words synonymous with the word **image**. That **image**, picture, or look is then used to further explain the direction or leaning of the poems in the given section. It also helps to show some of my Father's **image** on an area of my life. This is not "Rocket Science" I try to save that for my other work. In this way I believe that the poems each follow the overarching theme of **image**.

This anthology represents the variations and degrees of freedom and growth of my writing since the early 80's. For over 30 years I have written about work, church, the word, God, society, friends and family. In it I believe that I have found a way to give voice to both joy and pain. Yet find a way to express some of the nuances of the plan, purpose and handiwork of the Lord.

The plan is to actually introduce you to some of my most valued words and poems along the way of each chapter. I also like to think that some of the poetic works will not need an introduction. Time will tell.

Finally, before I had the opportunity to publish this book, I had a "Life Event". I like to think that I am stronger and more focused since it happened. It actually inspired me to stop wasting time and start pouring out my thoughts, gifts, and ideas. Previous to the poetic words following, please read, Porcelain Man or Bonus Man.

Porcelain Man or Bonus Man

"Mr. Bosley it appears that you have just experienced a **Heart Episode**". What becomes my method and practice for dealing with life? So now what do I do, the doctor was telling me I've just had a heart attack, how do I live? Since so very much has been said about our attitudes and how they literally **create** the difference in our lives I determined that I would use this same advice to help leverage my future. The reason for this is that I realized that I needed to do something to help anchor my attitude both for and "in" the future. If I don't set my sights on the future, thoughts of every breath becoming my last could get troubling very quick. I recalled from a recent good read, ***"Change or Die"***[1] that if I don't do some proactive things that **denial** will set in and I will likely lose all of the skilled work that the doctors have done. I hope that you agree that life is too short to leave our mental programming to chance variables.

Just before my "Heart Episode", I had just attended the **2009 Columbus Area Homeschoolers Graduation**. I sat on the dais with now Governor, Mike Pence, waiting to give the Invocation, Remarks and Blessing. During my remarks one of the things that I told the graduates was that they needed to be aware of their environment. So I listened to my own advice. I listened and watched those that came to see me or that sent messages to me during my brief hospital stay. I heard the cautions, advice and warnings of doctors, nurses, friends and family. I heard the words and prayers of encouragement, edification, peace, and comfort. I heard from the sympathetic as well as the empathetic. This all affected my perspective, and while I believe that a rigorous thought process has shaped this view I realize that it will require the passage of time to validate. My view is that I can approach the balance of my life with either of two perspectives. I can approach it as a **"Porcelain Man"** or as a **"Bonus Man"**.

A **Porcelain Man** will live for the future. He will save himself for some date yet to be determined. I examined that there are many porcelain articles, or items in our lives. During my hospital stay I shared this story with visitors; it is from a new book that I am reading. They say that Mark Twain told of a man that died and met St Peter in heaven. *"**The man always had one question that he had wondered about throughout his life and asked, "Who was the greatest general of all time?" St Peter said, "That's easy, the man right over there." The man replied, maybe you misunderstood me, I knew that man and he was a common laborer." "That's right said, St Peter, He would have been the greatest general, if he had been a general.""*** A Porcelain Man fears damage. Currently, I am looking at the little sugar bowl that sits on our kitchen table. It looks good on the outside. To be truthful, there are limits to how we use it. There are concerns that it may crack, scuff or chip. As a **Porcelain Man** I would be much the same. I would look "good" on the outside. There would be all of these limits about what I would do and not do. Places and things that I would get involved in and not because of what "**could**" happen. Ultimately, I'd be saving what's inside for some far off future date that is not promised to me.

Then of course there is the **"Bonus Man"**. This is a much more empowering perspective. Especially, when one examines the raw data on the number of **"Heart Episodes"** that many people have especially on Monday mornings only to end as a terminal statistic. As a **Bonus Man** I recognize the frailty of life and that being given more time on the planet is a rare and unique gift that is not afforded to all, **Bonus**! This is not to say that I would not govern any of my life by the wisdom of my doctors, and appreciate the significant potencies of the prescribed medicines. Again as I shared earlier, this would run me a foul of the information I learned from ***Change or Die***. The doctors have said switch to a low fat/low sodium diet, take these pills everyday and get more exercise. And I fully intend to be a model patient in these regards, **Bonus**! The road that the ***Porcelain Man* diverges** from the **Bonus Man** on is the future versus the present. As a Porcelain Man I would hold my cards and opinions for some future bet, gamble, or investment. As a **Bonus Man** every chance to **"double down"** or bet on myself would be done with an eye towards, ***"maybe this is why I'm here".***

So then who is the extra life in this individual a **Bonus** for? Truly, that remains to be seen but I am trying to live to the glory of my Creator. Right now, I am enjoying my own company as well as that of my family. I choose to believe that this new clock is for everyone that has the opportunity to tap into my thoughts, ideas, views or opinions. These first few weeks the dog will find that she has a unique opportunity to experience my time, talents and perspective. As the days wind on I hope to widen my sphere of influence. My prayer is that hopefully someday down the line you can think back on this time and say, **Bonus**!

Sincerely,
David C. Bosley 5/31/09

1. Created In God's Image

Genesis 1:27 So God created man in his own image, in the image of God created he him; male and female created he them.

Image: form; appearance; semblance: We are all created in God's image.

The Power of Prophetic Words

Last night December 20th was a wild night! But the Holy Spirit won the victory. It started earlier in the day, with some slight indigestion. However, there was so much more going on. I realized that I was going to an anniversary service later that evening and would want to give remarks, yet now had a terrible physical situation. So I sat down and with great pains, so I thought, searched the language to make a poem for my friend, Suffragan Bishop Derek Lamont Jefferson.

I essentially put the finishing touches on it at 5:49pm, as my wife Charlene and I made our way to the garage to first pick up our daughter Christen for this 7:00pm service.

Charlene had just returned home from a visit to Cincinnati. We made it to the church at about 7:10pm or so and found our seats in the congregation, as they were in the praise service.

Eventually, Bishop Jefferson and an entourage made their way out and I was asked to join them on the pulpit. I was sat next to the Master of Ceremony (MC). I had to excuse myself once during praise service to deal with the physical issue, which had become unruly, but eventually made my way back to my seat.

Several great speakers were asked to give remarks and one of them mentioned how growing up and playing church, over the years, helped to make Bishop Jefferson into a pastor. This struck me, because I say the same in my poem, yet I did not grow up with Bishop Jefferson over the years. I have come to know him because his Brother-in-law was my pastor while we lived in Indianapolis for a number of years. So I saw the hand of God in what I originally thought were just my words. So I was inspired to touch the MC, "I have a poem if there is time and if appropriate."I said. He looked over his notes then mentioned, "Sure, during Remarks".

Then it was on! Bishop Jefferson took the podium and called the names of several pastors, including myself, which were to make remarks. I lined up with the rest. At this point I began laboring in my mind, do I abbreviate my poem in the interest of time? Do I say the entire word to have it prophetically affect the atmosphere, the church, the pastor and the guest? I determine that I will read it in its entirety, though a bit rushed. I admit that while satisfied that I "Got it out there", I wasn't completely certain that it was prophetic at the time. So I just chalked it up as another time I could have done better. "Let's head home", I said.

We made a couple of stops before dropping off Christen, "Nothing to eat for me, thanks!" Then the light drizzle of rain, seemed to turn into a "combat zone in water" as we made it to the expressway. Maybe I was driving a bit fast, OK, I was. But I had a situation and had to get home. Then a car that was behind me speedily got in front of me and slowed a bit, but remained in front all the way to our exit, about an hour later. I finally maneuvered into the slow lane to exit. This car did the same and then just went on past the exit. I now recognize him as like an angel, keeping me safe and keeping my speed down.

Once home Charlene and I went into our "bedtime" routine. We were both well worn from the day's events. I made it to bed first, but quickly awoke with the chills. Charlene suggested some Tylenol™. She brought it and had the sense to pray for us both once she got in bed.

I wrestled with sleep. I tussled to keep the covers over me from the dread of cold. I eventually awoke speaking in tongues. The chills and what may have been a fever broke. Then the Spirit spoke to me. I had such a battle writing the poem earlier because our language is dirty, old, incomplete, and fraught with spiritual gaps and holes. I am reminded of **Isaiah 6:5** ***"Then said I, Woe is me! for I am undone; because I am a man of unclean lips, and I dwell in the midst of a people of unclean lips: for mine eyes have seen the King, the LORD of hosts"***. If God's children's lips were unclean then, imagine them now!

I was told that the poems are a gift of the Spirit, and often they have the ability to speak **prophetically**! I got out of bed realizing that last night was a spiritual battle. A battle the enemy did not want me to win, because I picked up a new tool or gift for the souls benefit.

I look back and notice that I have had better success when I am moved to capture a poetic work or song from a sleep, or base the words on The Word, or scripture. I have told others that when I am awakened out of sleep with a poem or word it is as if I am listening in on the songs or conversation of angels. Earlier, I had shared with my wife while she was still in Cincinnati, that the Lord had blessed me to write another poem, titled: **Grace For Grace**. That poem was based on various New Testament scriptures on **grace**.

Lamar Campbell and The Spirit of Praise, was there at Bishop Jefferson's service and sung immaculately! One of the songs they performed, although created by Detrick Haddon, He's Able, ministered to Charlene and I as we battled our way home through the water. Isn't it special that in the scriptures water is associated to the Spirit and the Word of God, yet the enemy thought that he could use it against us! Don't give up on God and he won't give up on you...He's Able!

True Life

True Life is composed of those who are chosen.
And my reason for life is not to reproduce strife.
No, my cause I have found, while I'm yet above ground,
It is to spread the word of God all around.

2. A Thought Before We Begin

Genesis 50:20 But as for you, ye thought evil against me; but God meant it unto good, to bring to pass, as it is this day, to save much people alive.

Thought, a consideration or reflection: The thought of death terrified her.

New Beginnings

This is it. I pray that you find this expression of me worth the read. My highest prayer is that you will find something in here that you call "good" because it affects you. The kind of affect that I am aiming for is to affect the brain, or more specifically the mind.

I'd like to make it clear right out of the gate that another inspiration of mine to do this book is the great words I have heard from others. There are some truly great writers, whether of poems, stories or speeches. Some writers that have especially moved me, in no particular order, are:

- Dr. Martin Luther King
- W.E.B. Dubois
- William Shakespeare
- Dr. Suess
- Langston Hughes
- Nikki Giovanni
- E.E. Cummings
- Dudley Randall

Of course there are many other great writers out there but these are all gifted. I salute each and everyone that dares to push thoughts through the written or spoken word. Some may even recall that I find it only like God, that someone like me would dare utter language in public given my early and teenage sheer fear of public speaking. In my inner city high school class of over 600 graduating seniors I was elected, The Shyest! The picture is of my brother Marty and I. I guess no one in high school thought that I would be writing a book.

My Dad, Joseph was pretty creative. I like to think that this was one of the impacts from my nurturing that blessed me to become an engineer. As seen from the Dedication that the creative writing and the way I use my words came mostly from my Mom, Leotha. Now to cap it all off God is pretty well known for His creative prowess. So claiming my writing as a gift from God drives a required action from me. I once told a group of children who did a Christmas play based on my first book, "**Love Came Down At Christmas Time**"[2], that a gift is not a gift until you give it. Therefore, since this writing is at least one of my gifts, I have to get it out there. "If you can't say Amen say, Duck!"

Begin Anew:

Begin anew; now is the right time to just go out and do it
For all the stuffy, stuff that's old, "Just New It!"

The relationships that are worn over years of time,
Recreate them again by applying your mind.

You say, "The love is gone and she won't do it",
Love is worth the risk my friend, "Just New It!"

"It's hard to teach an ole dog a new set of tricks",
The hard part is to quit whining, and then begin it.

Get up and put one foot in front of the other,
Besides he ain't "Heavy" dear heart, that's your brother.

Change or Die, conveys a message that's not hard to construe,
But health and life studies find that nine out of ten often do.

Many make a great start and they run out of gas,
They begin in a flash but in denial they crash!

They deny the reason for making a change,
They deny the motive of a life rearranged.

Then all this denial breaks down like soup,
That clogs up the psyche and turns it to goop.

This happens a bunch if we start with the "How",
The "**Why**" is more attractive for motivating the "Now".

I changed for my family and I changed for my friends,

So I can serve God a little longer, is my ultimate end.

But whether for health, or spirit, it's all up to you.
Just begin my friend to remake the old new.
"Just New It!"

3. A Copy For The Children

Deuteronomy 17:18 And it shall be, when he sitteth upon the throne of his kingdom, that he shall write him a copy of this law in a book out of that which is before the priests the Levites:

Copy: an imitation, reproduction, or transcript of an original: a copy of a famous painting.

It seemed like it use to be easy. Growing up appears much harder now. Which by extension suggest that Mothering may be harder today as well.

I came across this very appropriate article several years ago. I think it is relevant today.

***Wednesday, May 2, 2007*[5]**

Mom's 2007 salary: $138K

The work of a stay-at-home mother has an annual monetary value of $138,095, up 3 percent from last year, according to a survey out today.
Those are some findings from the seventh annual Mom Salary Survey issued by Salary.com, a Waltham compensation software and consulting firm.

How much are stay-at-home moms worth?
If paid the salary of the equivalent work that a stay-at-home mother performs, a woman would earn $138,095, the company said.
And if a working mother regarded parenting as a second job, that second job would command an annual salary of $85,939; that's on top of the money she earns in the work place, Salary.com said.
More than 80 percent of employers are actively recruiting mothers re-entering the work force, and among the reasons is that mothering hones such as work-place skills and virtues as multitasking, compassion, dependability, and people skills, Salary.com said.
"Mothers are not only talented; they're experienced managers, motivators, decision makers and client specialists after spending time in both the work force and as a mother," Salary.com senior vice president Bill Coleman said in a statement.

Yes, mothers are not paid enough for what they do. And children have it a bit tougher today in many ways than when I was growing up. The picture above is two of my brothers (Marty and Tommy) and I. Kids today have access and opportunity to many more things and places to make bad decisions.

In the final analysis this section suggests that, Mothers are not paid enough for all that they do. Then it suggests that we adults need to do more for Every Child.

A Mother Is

Matchless poise, grace, and beauty,
And every day she does her duty.
This is who your mother is.
Watch her as she handles her biz.

Mend a heart, or wipe a tear.
The hand of God, we hold so dear.
If you have a story to tell,
her ears will listen and listen well.

They can even read your mind.
The only thing they need is time,
And a minute or two in your eyes.
They know what's up, don't tell no lies.

Runny noses and runny bottoms.
Chicken pox, mumps, they know when you caught em
The day, the month, the year, she knows,
even the last time you stubbed your toe.

A smile, a laugh, a forlorn look.
It's mothers yall they wrote the book.
Now God knows the hairs upon your head,
But it's Momma's jurisdiction if you dye them red.

A Virtuous woman in the marketplace,
But not if you have a dirty face.
Spit and a hanky will make you clean,
And don't you dare create a scene.

She's got shoes that fly like boomerangs,
Watch as Mamma does her thing.
Cause when Moms does it, the job gets done.
You're blessed if you ever had you one.

She's up late at night. Sometimes early in the day,
But if someone needs mindin, by the bed she'll stay.
Just within ear shot is where she'll light,
And if there's a need, she's there all night.

Unspoken words, unwritten laws.
Don't try to stop her when she's found her cause.
A hand that knows just where it hurts.
Lips kiss boo-boos and skin that's burnt.

Arms that pick us up when we fall,
And ears that hear us when we call.
A lap that rocks our pain away.
A bosom to hug us when there's no words to say.

A mind to have us do our best.
And a heart to love us till we know we're blessed.
Not enough words to say it all.
We needed an angel with us, so Moms got the call.

For Every Child

Matthew 6:20 says we should store up for ourselves treasures in heaven, where nothing can break through and steal. Then verse 21 comes along with a new paradigm to reveal.

It says that wherever your treasure is, that's where your heart will be too. Cause wherever you put your money says that thing is important to me and you.

Consider that, in what is thought to be the richest nation there'll ever be. The way we spend our money reveals preventing poverty is not a priority.

Poverty is a lack of the socially acceptable material possessions. It is the state of absence of money an essential needed in privation.

We should care because poverty affects all of us and most of all the child. And research shows it affects their well being and leaves their learning somewhat wild.

The National Center for Children in Poverty, states, 21% live below the line. And by where we store our treasure, for most of us that is just fine!

A '96 Fordham University report says that children and young people unfortunately suffer the most. But it is about our stealth bombers and millionaire sports stars that we all seem to boast.

When in 2009 social lack approached the '60s levels we declared War on Poverty. And Government agencies provided millions of aid to Americans that did not come for free.

Yet typically the objective of any given war is to be the victor and to win. Yet while millions of dollars have been given this war to date it sees no end.

In 2011 extreme poverty, households living on less than 2 bucks per day, was double that of '96. One might scream 1.5 million households, including 2.8 million children, we better get that fixed!

Can't we see that, low wages and unstable employment intro new challenges for a child's learning. Because a parent has enough to worry about when minimum wage is all they are earning.

In 2012 the Census said poverty had spread from 14 to 16% you see, the pain of these numbers was 20% were children, the highest since '93.

Lately to this mix comes, Standards-Based Reform and the Poverty Gap: Lessons for "No Child Left Behind". But when will others get involved is the question that resonates in my mind!

"Will Standards-Based Reform in Education Help Close the Poverty Gap?" If we simply think a study will bring the solution then we've met the age old trap.

The solution will not come until thousands decide to pray. And then a thousands thousand decide they will help make a better day.

When hundred's find their voice, my friend, and say, "We will roll up our sleeves!" "Just to be a part of a community that, Lights it up!, whenever there's a need.

To be a part of a greater whole that gives cash, whenever they lend a **hand**! And that makes a point to give it deep, as they channel, that bush stuck ram.

There are more numbers that I could throw out enough to make you wince and even cry. But why waste time on more numbers and then stand idly by?

There are programs in this community to stem the present threat. They do a great work on a great cause and haven't given up yet.

I realize that my impassioned pleas may sometimes come off wild. But this is a plea made from the heart because it's for every child.

4. A Figure For Virtuous Women

Deuteronomy 4:16 Lest ye corrupt yourselves, and make you a graven image, the similitude of any figure, the likeness of male or female,

Figure: form or shape, as determined by outlines or exterior surfaces: ***to be round, square, or cubical in figure.***

I set out to find a picture of an industrious woman and I was blessed to find this picture of Aunt Marsha, Mom's sister. Growing up as well as now she has been a blessing and a delight for my siblings and I. She sings like a canary.

God is very particular about folk trying to set forth an image or figure that represents Him. He says in Isaiah, I am God to whom will you compare me. The key scripture above indicates that in the law God gave strict directions to avoid setting forth a manufactured image for the purposes of worship.

Never-the-less, I am cognizant of several beautiful mothers of the church, like Aunt Marsha, that live or have lived a simple life that basically focused on the figure of Jesus. That simple yet, powerful idea, seems to dynamicize their walk and years of service in the church.

The poems in this chapter were all written to honor blessed mothers. Know that I have been blessed to meet many more than there are poems here. Let's just say that the poems that you'll find in this section are representative of the fine and God blessed mothers in the church and in the community.

Some of them have children of their own. Some have no birth children. They all were outstanding pillars in the church; as I said some were pillars in their communities as well. These are mature women that seemed to put a loving arm around someone to help and nurture them to be better than maybe they thought they could be. Bless you mothers, you have done virtuously.

NATURALLY NEVER ALONE

Her wit was quick, Her mind was strong,
And you soon knew it if you didn't belong.

And if you didn't belong, you knew not to stay,
A few choice words would have you on your way.

Not to say that Aunt Nug the lady, was a little too rough,
Cause she could often speak her mind without gettin gruff.

When you live to better than 103,
some things come to you naturally.

I liked how, she'd break it down and with simplicity she'd say,
things others find complex in a much more interesting way,

"She made it an art to simply state her case,
too bad if the truth just busted you all up in your face.

She was special and showed her anger just like she showed her love,
For instance, Aunt Nug loved her some Jesus, his tender mercies from above.

She also loved her precious family and demonstrated it through their care,
They were spread about all over you know, she had family just about everywhere.

"What you know about Jesus Bostic", His name is Bosley, Dot would say,

"I know the man's name girl," That was just her way.

Vergie Mae Moore has left us now to find a better home,
"What you know about Jesus Bostic", I know she'll never be alone!
Love you: Aunt Nug

Daughters of Zelophehad

*Here is a little **story** about the daughters of **Zelophehad**,*
*These five **sisters** had a problem that soon made them **mad**.*
They said that, **Dad is dead**, *and here lays his **land**,*
*But they won't allow **us** to have it, because we aren't a **man**.*
*They said it would **be one thing** if Dad had been very **bad**,*
*But he walked the **straight and narrow** ever since he was a **lad**.*
Moses brought their **concerns** *straight to the* **LORD,**
*The daughters speak **right**, they are a fivefold **chord.***
*God also said, they **speak the truth** in the things that they **say**,*
*So we gotta give it to the **ladies**, when they say it right, **today**!*

From Numbers the 27th chapter

GIVE GOD THE BEST

I didn't come by just to sit and see, while the rest decides what's gonna be,

But no way your duties are you gon shirk, and all lay around and watch me work.

So all you folk get off the bench for the Lord abhors the sluggard's stench,

So don't hold up services till others come and just stand around all looking glum.

Let's drive on forward and slack not your reins, because it's the slothful that GOD disdains.

Keep your hands busy is what "THE PREACHER" tells me, cause we're not finished from what I can see.

Now I know that building a Church takes some time but you can't build it all inside your mind.

It takes some sweat and some muscle too, so roll up your sleeves cause we ain't near through.

Lay all your shoulders to the wheel, I've done my share to help clear the field.

And she did it well for all her years her words of faith rebuking fears.

Now she's gone to take her rest, her simple message "GIVE GOD YOUR BEST."

Love You: Mother Viona Mathis

A Great, Grand, Mother

I will bless the LORD at all times: his praise shall continually be in my mouth.
Everywhere that I go I will think of Him, whether East, West, North or South.

My soul shall make her boast in the LORD: the humble shall hear it, and be glad.
As a Church Missionary I will serve the Lord, no closer friend could be had.

O magnify the Greatness of my God with me, and together let us lift up his name.
Through Sunday School I've taught saints all about Him if they don't serve Him now it's a shame.

I searched out the LORD and He heard me, and deliverance came to me from my fears.
Now in Faith I walk in His ways my child, I've learn that His Word is good through the years.

They looked unto God and were lit up: and their faces were no more ashamed.
Since Believers In Christ that's my experience He'll bless those that trust in His Name.

This poor man cried, and Jesus heard him, and saved him from all of his troubles.
Whenever I've fallen He picks me up, He never leaves His kids in the rubble.

The angel of the LORD camps out very near here, around all

of them that fear Him.
The Host of Heaven fight for God's word y'all, the enemies forces are no match for them.

O taste and see that the LORD is good: blessed is a woman found in true Motherhood.
A Great Grand Mother, she's done her best you know, to train her kids up like she should.

And she's done a great job of it a Virtuous lady with Greater Love Temple her home,
Its plain to see that she loves Jesus, and from His arms she'll never ever roam.
With Love
To Mother Alice Elliott

The Tides That Swell

Gwendolyn is gone from here.
No more that mischievous grin we hold so dear.
That grin meant that a request was near.
We will cherish it still, when it's gone from here.

On the "Pulse of the Morning" we must give praise.
Giving honor where it's due, is what the Good book says.
And so we thank her for all she's done,
from early rise, till setting sun.

Her efforts make her worthy of this display.
"Excuse me I have to take this call", was just her way.
Then she'd return with progress to report.
The "multitask dance" was just her sport.

Second Baptist we know will miss her too,
once her Saturn SUV has gone from view.
The community as well will miss ole Blue.
Pennsylvania St no more, she'll bid it adieu.

NAACP will need prayer and some strong direction,
Lacking now the adrenaline of Gwen and her poised interjections.
She had us at the right place, at just the right time.
Hope all those dates weren't just in her mind?

Gwen is headed to sandy beaches and conch shells.
With salty air and tides that swell.
No more Carson's or local government work,
She'll find a sturdy lounge chair with which to flirt.

And rest she will until comes that call,
"We need her back!" From one and all!
To show one last time just how it's done.
No, you blessed us well, now go have some fun!

Gwendolyn Short Wiggins

Virtuously

Mrs. Louise Bosley, Queen that you are, For today's celebration we have traveled from far. Others have come over hill, and over dale. To share in the flowers to this virtuous female.

Her virtue is a term that I do not take lightly
I'll present you examples and share them politely.
Yes, she's known in the market that is a fact.
As she styles the lockets of hair jet black.

Jet black, long, short, red, auburn or gray,
She can make you look stylish in a virtuous way.
In the Assemblies of God she is known too,
Because a little praise for Jesus just will not do!

And since the Word says, "Faith without works is dead."
"She's a worker in the church." I've heard it been said.
Strength and honor are her clothing, as she's "Dressed to the Nine's."
And I must say Mrs. Louise, "You sure do look fine."

Many daughters have done virtuously, but thou excellest them all.
A blessing going out, coming in, summer, winter, spring, or fall.
So I present you your flowers as I share of your fame. You are blessed with virtue, cause you are blessed in Jesus Name!

5. The Likeness That Clears Problems

Genesis 5:1 This is the book of the generations of Adam. In the day that God created man, in the likeness of God made he him;

Likeness: the semblance or appearance of something; guise: to assume the likeness of a swan.

The picture is of Deacon Joe Bosley, my Dad along with two of my brothers and I. Deacon Bosley would remind me that there is a faithful saying, "Trouble don't last always!" I believe that after God created Adam and he fell, that there was a hope yet found for mankind. I believe that the hope for mankind was found in the 2nd Adam, that man Jesus. The scriptures let us know that he came in the "likeness" of God, full of power.

In this chapter I have placed several poems that give me a renewed perspective when I have been faced with problems or challenges. They even have empowering titles as they deal with empowering themes: Brotherhood, Praise, Friends, and Grace.

If you are going through a rough patch maybe you just need to remember that God Inhabits Praise. "Problems... Trouble don't last always!"

A Taste of Brotherhood

Oh taste and see that the Lord is good, and that His Spirit dwells in Brotherhood.

Babel knows well of it for the people's mind's were one, So that only the move of God prevented what they had begun.

Rebekah abused Brotherhood in the raising of her sons, with her foolish deception trying to pick God's chosen one.

Obadiah made illustration of it as Edom' s prophecy, Esau' s fallout from Rebekah as he shunned a brother in need.

Theophilus knows well of it cause Dr. Luke penned it out, as he wrote of holy stories of Brothers that had clout.

How good and how pleasant it is, Is what Psalm 133 has to say. Portraying that Brotherhood is a Holy way.

Elijah knew of Brotherhood's taste, but thought Jezebel killed all but him, Until God reassured his soul that there were dozens left of them.

Reconciliation of new brothers is our duty you must see Ambassadors of this heavenly title is our ministry.

Holiness you see is required of a Brotherly heart. But if iniquity and sins abound they'll keep us all

Oil of the Spirit is the ointment we must desire, cause if Brotherly love doesn't continue we will have quenched God's Holy Fire.

Obedience also I must note is in this blessed mix. So if you think sacrifice will do, Ya better get that fixed.

Divine anointing from above sums up this heavenly taste, cause when we show our brothers love we know God is in this place.

Be Strong, Brother Strong: Remix

Be strong and of a good courage, fear not, and be not afraid,
For the LORD thy God he is with you, and will always be your aid.
He goes before you and will not forsake you, He will always help you prevail.
Just trust Him for the victory, Have faith cause His glory will not fail.

Only be thou strong and very courageous, when you think about God's holy law
Just as Moses presented it to Pharaoh, remember the mighty miracles he saw.
This Bible book stays before us always, as we meditate herein day and night,
That you observe to do what is written herein: cause it makes our lives come out alright

Turn not from it to the right hand or to the left, so you'll prosper whithersoever you go.
This book of the law shall not depart out of thy mouth; but meditate for your faith to grow.
Truly Christ has blessed your work in the kingdom and anointed you with fire.
He has blessed you from day to day and granted your heart to be blessed with desire.

Be ye strong therefore and let it never be said, that your hands have become weak.

For your good work shall be rewarded, if the Lord is the first one you seek!
We then that are strong in our deeds, ought to bear the infirmities of the weak.
And not please ourselves with pride, just as we are to remain humble and meek.

Many have used their strength through faith, to subdue ungodly kingdoms,
Others have stopped unrighteousness, and repelled the evil spirits that bring them.
Others out of weakness were made strong, and even waxed valiant in fight,
Others turned the armies of the aliens around, so that rather than battle they turn in flight.

But you my dear brother if you remain strong, will be an above average fellow,
And that strength from the Lord will give you quiet reserves, so that even with issues you are mellow.
So now that you have matriculated and learned what the Lord now wants you to see.
Just continue to use what God has blessed you with, to set the captive souls you find free!

Friends and Family Day

Friends and Family Day a time we can all take part,
A time when even us city folk can learn to do something smart

A time for young and old to take some time with friends,
To celebrate in fellowship before the church service begins

A time for aunties, "Uncs", and cousins, sis, and even "mamma-nem",
The neighbors, and other Believer's in Christ, and sit down and share a meal with all of them.

A time to see that before the church, God 1st created the family.
From one man and one woman the Bible says we were all blessed to be.

All these folk the Lord had made, then settled in the Valley of Shinar,
Wasn't till God confused their language that some decided to travel far.

Travelling far and wide some families ended up in Columbus,
Others just passing through, still take the time to walk among us.

Then there's our friends, we note them all too dear and plenteous to count,
That take the time to fellowship and show what true friendship is about.

This is the time, this is the place to share a laugh, a hug, and

shake a hand.
Remember it's a Celebration yall, for boys, girls, every woman and every man.

There's much I could say about this blessed day and all those that participate.
But there's food involved so I'll wrap this up and work on my, "To Go" plate.

Poetic Sampling of Me

I heard it, a tinny, grand hiccup of the mind
That's what keeps me from fallin behind.

I should know better, than to get tripped in their words
This is crazy, no a better way to say it is, absolutely absurd

I'm driving to make it to what looks like a better place
I'm losing all composer and my little piece of grace

Subsiding from the touch that seems to set me back,
Giving up on vain Attitudes, watch the lights, fade to black

Words and memories all a muster and billowy grey,
False hope, weak knees, look up, finding a way.

All just a thought on the nuance of things that could be,
Not too much, just a little bit of the reflections of me!

[7]

What The University of Dayton Means To Me

Freshmen to Dayton just coming in, and people getting settled to their new homes again.
Parties, late nights and up early for my class, I've just peeped out a foxy new Flyer lass.

Rushin, Smokers, tell what they're about, pledging Chokers that frats got clout,
Little sisters, "skee-weet", "ooh-oot" what's that noise, sounds like the ladies are wolf calling boys.
What UD means to me.

Kennedy Union stops between bells, The Soaps are on, pledging's swell.
Higher Learning here, new thoughts start to form, Can't fit my big head, inside my small dorm.

Distinguished Speakers, usher gigs, kicking bad habits like smokin cigs.
Bowling, gaming, highest score, Christmas on Campus, now it's snowing more.
What UD means to me.

KU quick stop can't be late, she's off at 7, ask for a date.

Boll Theater this seat is mine, you can open your eyes now, it's
"Young Frankenstein"[8].

Apartment roomies give me space, an upper classman it's like
my own place,
Cookies baking, oatmeal scotchies cause I love the taste, and
peanut butter too! None here to waste.
What UD means to me.

Dr Wolf and Professor Rooney makes our day, Chem lab and
Electronics seem like play.
Principles of Management and Macro Ec', Can't see you till
late, my schedules a wreck.

Friendships made, some last forever, but others we will see no
more, never.
Profs and staff were special too, Checking us out through the
year, love to hear what we do.
What UD means to me.

The Law Library, Ghetto, and Founder's Hall, so much to
mention, can't think of it all.
Some ideas come from worlds away, and affect our psyche
during work and play.

Some brothers are really brothers now, many preachers of
Christ; Looking back one never imagines the subtle shifts of
life.
Red and Blue but hearts of Gold, they support us thru the
down days as we grow old.
What UD means to me.

34 years ago you became my friend, enjoying the studies there seemed like it would never end.
Now husband and wife and yet we still date, Looking back on fond memories, wasn't campus life great!

What UD means to me.

GOD INHABITS PRAISE

Angels bow before Him, Heaven and Earth adore Him.
He made a world and set it free.
GOD inhabits praise you see.

Jericho knows about Him, He touched their walls you see,
and Pharaoh knows His power, He set Moses' people free.

Praising Him wins victories, because Praise is in His name.
Praise Him for His blood and you too will know His fame.

The sounds of rushing mighty winds from a distance may sound like cheers,
For the Holy Spirit in tongues you see, sets saints free from their fears.

Praise Him when you're able, praise Him while you're weak.
When you're down without a prayer it's His face that you should seek.

Cause troubles are bound to happen, but don't fret, cry or despair.
And don't bow your head and lose your faith because you think the world unfair.

Know that slip-ups sometimes happen so lock into this simple phrase.
"WHEN YOU'RE LOST WITHOUT A HOPE GOD INHABITS PRAISE!"

Grace For Grace

Grace is of God a simple virtue as it flows down from above,
Sent down as a godsend as an emissary of His love.

Receptors of faith, that it might be by grace; sent in parabolic
distribution to affect the whole human race.

Establishing a promise that it might be sure to all the seed; and
lift us up one and all, wherever there is a need.

Description of His promise now full of grace and truth.
Blessing all who cherish it both the aged and the youth.

It ushers in spirit gifts differing according to their grace, and
graces all appointments as we are empowered in this place.

Do we seize it, do we dare it, let it be said now grace for grace.
The enemy would foreswear it, cannot stop it, catch a case.

Sin's accountant reckoned of grace, now of debt, no longer
owed. Created great grace with great power and of His loving
mercy showed.

Grace through the redemption that is only found in Jesus
Christ: Or shall we continue in sin, that grace may abound and
remain forever locked in strife?

We'll not live any longer in sin, since the old man is in the
ground! I'm standing tall according to the riches of his grace
and the new power that I've found.

We are children walking in abundance of grace in a vessel mortal true, But this vessel has a future living in a glorious body new.

We have read the word of His grace, which is able to build you up, and it will renew you to once you drink it from salvation's blessed cup.

Come my friend and drink this cup of the grace of the Lord Jesus Christ. The Holy Communion is this cup in his blood is found new life.

We are a remnant according to the very election of grace. Called to be his saints dear hearts receiving Grace through faith.

Risen now disciples to receive, what we believed through grace we won: Grace and peace from God our Father, and the Lord Jesus Christ His only son.
Grace For Grace.

6. The Refiner's Reflection for Dreamers

Mal 3:3** **And he shall sit as a <u>refiner</u> and purifier of silver: and he shall purify the sons of Levi, and purge them as gold and silver, that they may offer unto the LORD an offering in righteousness.

Refiner: to free, or improve or perfect by pruning or polishing.

The picture is of the Dr. Martin Luther King, Jr. Memorial[3] in Washington, D.C. Truly, he was one of the world's great Dreamers.

I love the passage from Malachi. I have had an opportunity to study early metal working. It informed me that when the silver worker worked on a crucible of molten silver that they only knew it was pure when they could look into it and see their own reflection. Surely, The Lord as our Refiner is looking for his own image in us as he works us. Of course if the silver is not completely purified a little more heat would be added and the silver agitated to cause any impurities to work to the surface and be wiped off.

Certainly there are ***dreamers*** in this world that have seemed to reflect so much of our Lord's character that you just know that they have a special anointing. In some we have to realize that their anointing was for a season. Whatever the case they reflect so much of God's image that many find it hard not to sit up and take notice. This chapter is committed to saying a good word about the ***dreamers*** I have known.

Come See A Man

Come see a man that knows what it takes, this can be attested
to by our own Bishop Jakes,
The true test of a Leader having what it takes, is to see who
will follow when they all know the stakes.

Bishop Ringer would share that he knew from the start that it
was the power of God that guided your heart.
A heart that is demonstrated for all around to see, as you love
on your flock with grace and honesty.

But it was Bishop Stephens that told me to come see a man
unique in his wardrobe, and unique in his stand.
With flash and a dap-ness that bespeak all your years, and the
courage to share the Word and then make it clear.

Now all of the Bishops and all of the Elders, and all of these
people have all come together.
All of these leaders have come together to say, that the course
that is set is a very blessed way.

This direction is the Lord's choosing and is recognized all
around as the seal of excellence that is Higher Ground!

Higher Ground Always Abounding Assemblies
Bless you **Bishop Sherman S. Watkins,**
Founder and Prelate
Higher Ground Always Abounding Assemblies, Inc.

The Dared Dream of Destiny

You have written down the vision, this is plain to see.
You didn't want ole Satan to get a hold of me.

The vision is now in books... for me to read a spell, to shore up my salvation in the Word and to keep my soul from hell.

The dream you had to spread the Word in the form of a Bible College, Now causes students 'round the world to excel in both wisdom and in knowledge.

"***Stay locked in the Process***", is what you continually told our souls, In time we were all blessed of God, who always had control.

You constantly plant and water leaders for the great harvest of our God, As long as they tarry for the Vision, whenever Jesus gives the nod.

More than 35 years, some lean, some fat, your Lord alone knows the number, because even in the lean you were also blessed of God whose covenant you're under.

The Time is now appointed, and the visions speaking to our hearts, The Anointing of the Spirit, we now know, has been here from the start.

"***11th Hour Workers***", is now the title of which we claim to be. Expressed to us in word sent of God, just to give us liberty.

See that wall, "***It's coming down***", is another dream that you shared, The pews too all heavy and blue now fit because you dared.

Dared to dream of the impossible for the church and yes community, Knowing your vision required the Hand of God for fulfillment of Destiny.

Your Labor Blesses Me

I esteem you both highly cause you watch for my very soul.
And I follow you as you follow Christ cause I know He's in control.

You're both my spiritual parents as I trust and obey.
Not only for your works sake, you should know this as we pray.

You rule your flock well a bishop with one wife, a virtuous 1st lady that blesses our church life.

Your labor has brought much fruit all must agree, But I above all else thank you both, for how your labor blesses me!

The Lad From Reelsville

A degreed Doctorate in Ministry and the founder of a Bible College, truly your eyes sparkle with the anointing of wisdom and knowledge.

Throughout your life great things God has done, and the Word of God tells us, ..He's only just begun".

For the many books you've written from the "Changing of The Guard" to "The Revelation of Jesus Christ". It is certainly self evident that the Hand of God has ruled your life.

And while on the path of God's rule there has been bitter and surely there has been sweet.

The Lad from Reelsville, IN may have been weary, but your Doctorate in Ministry is now complete!

Bishop Charles A. Sims In honor of the completing of your Doctorate in Ministry Degree

Just - Dream

The world's greatest treasure in paper and ink, are the
thoughts of a writer that causes us to think.
And this thinking does something that we consider quite rare,
if it causes a rustle and stir in the air.

These thoughts that are laid down are not what they seem,
they are the powerful expressions found in **"The Dream"**.
We thought a dream was a vapor and so darned ephemeral,
that it's only motivation would soon end up clearly terminal.

But **"The Dream"** had as its center and had as its core, the
power to persuade and so it carried so much more.
More power, more passion, more effect on a nation, than the
energies reflected in our country's celebration.
It had as its genesis an absolute and a moral ideal, which
tapped into a future though revolutionary and surreal.

An idea peaked by our sons and peaked by our daughters,
which said together we could help avoid the coming mindless
slaughter.
A slaughter that kills and steals all men's souls, that rampages
our hamlets and wrestles for control.

Control of a man and control of a mind, that would have
perpetuated slavery and to rights remained blind.
So **"The Dream"** spread like the raw fire of **inception**, and
became an imperative of heated moral indoctrination.

That's all my way of saying that **"The Dream"** had real power,
that caused it to stick to our psyches just like the scripture's
tower,
The tower we evaluate if we have the true grit to build, or is its
costs found too high and we not have the will.

All of these contemplations have fed into this vision, and illustrate that if we have the courage we can rise above derision.
Yes, Dr. King has shown we can do it if we dare, we can change the tide of centuries and go bout anywhere.

No state is our limit and <u>"No way"</u> is our taunt, because with the courage to dream we can do just what we ought.
So the platform of "***Oughtness***" today is our stage, the next step is yours to take, "**No**", it cannot be saved.

Or put up and preserved for some other rainy day, you must move interposition and procrastination out the way.
Some dream to have courage to do what they should, to speak out their first mind and not shriek from imagined hoods.

Imagined hoods of closed doors and possible closed hearts, but the closed become opened when we just do our part.
This part is within us a portion of our plan; it is fear that is not a part of the composition of a man.

Our part is easy when we do what's been deemed, God says it's a part of our make-up to have the courage to …Just Dream!

"Letter From A Birmingham Jail, A Simple Reprise"

re·prise, rɪˈpraɪz or; rəˈpriz, ***noun***
2.*Music.* **a.** a repetition. **b.** a return to the first theme or subject. (Today we call it the Remix)

NOTE: ***Birmingham was the largest city in Alabama with a population of approximately 225,000. During the 1950s and 1960s, Birmingham was one of the most segregated cities in the South with strict city ordinances that made it unlawful for different races to mix and mingle in almost all social settings.***

My Dear Dr. King:
"A Call for Unity", a message in response to **Protest** for change to come, Eight Alabama clergymen counter **Marches** with the voice of one. A league of eight now comes together with an easy view to share, "How dare you infuse and instigate, where we have called for prayer!"

We make an impassioned appeal for law, and order, and old fashioned common sense. We believe that change will come to racial problems if we discuss without pretense.

Perhaps it is while that you are stuck in jail that you will listen to why your **Marches** will fail.

My Dear Fellow Clergymen:
First my brothers I must admit, I've never seen a statute built to bless critics, Yet respond I must to you as men of goodwill, since you're sincere of heart and not rot with ill.

No, I'm not an outsider, how could I be, when the shores of this great land are what we call free. I have ties here and I was invited, please don't get agitated, and don't get excited.

I preach, "Thus saith the Lord", wherever I may go, sharing the gospel and never making a show. Injustice anywhere, is a threat everywhere; we are a network of mutuality. We also have ties to souls across the ocean, since they too aspire to destiny.

You seem to hate the protest, but embrace the appalling conditions! What good is so called freedom, if it never meets with fruition? You seem to enjoy the analysis of this rotten mess but lack the will to drive change. However, I am willing to drive to progress because I sense that it is within range.

There are **4 Steps** or **Phases** to every single nonviolent campaign: 1st there is a collection of the facts to determine if any injustices remain; Then 2nd there is the give and take of peaceful negotiation; Then 3rd the removal of prideful motivations and self-purification.

It is only after these first three steps that we can lock in on Step Four; so when we engage in Direct Action campaigns we are focused to the core. Birmingham is the state's worse racial offender and leads in individual offenses. Its history of broken promises and false hope indicate a lack of moral senses.

So where hope is lost it appears that Direct Action is now required, the moral conscience of a nation to be our judge, against dogs, water hoses, and sometimes fire. Purged as with hyssop to take both blows and the raw ordeal of jail, Bull Connor Commissioner of Police, thinks he can be integration's death nail.

Sit-ins, marches, and demonstrations are used to drive existing tension, all through nonviolent instigation, negotiation by peaceful confrontation. Direct Action helps men rise from the prejudice of a self-enraptured mind, to the Majestic heights of understanding and the brotherhood of all mankind.

Our Direct Action program creates a crisis-packed situation, one ambiguously froth with pitfalls that screams for dialogue and inspired negotiation.

Unfortunately, even the new city administration cast its vote for segregation, two sides of the same proverbial coin, and no closer to integration.

Groups more immoral than individuals is what we've been reminded, and that the leopard would change its spots, we were not so naively blinded.

Many of you seem to shout, "Why could we not just wait!" A "well timed, "Wait!" always meant "Never", like watching non-drying paint. Even more because "justice delayed is justice soon denied." Like seeing tears all well up in a grieving mother's eye.

Where was the "Wait", when vicious mobs lynched our mothers and our fathers." Where was the "Wait", when "**frienemies"** sat down and drowned our sisters and our brothers. Where was the "Wait" as hate-filled policemen kicked and killed our Uncles and our Aunts? Where is the "Wait" that persecutes the demons that today go uncaught?

"An unjust law is no law at all", St. Augustine has said. But you suggest we just wait or hold our breath perhaps till we're all dead? An unjust law degrades human personality, and then distorts the soul, and relegates persons to the status of things of which another can take control.

When you see the majority of 20 million brothers smothering in an airtight cage of Negro poverty, it causes you to wonder if the American Dream applies to **me**?

And then you find your tongue all twisted as you try so hard to explain, to your six-year-old daughter why she can't ride the Fun-town train. You can't go to the public amusement park honey, that place wasn't made for you, we have to find a special place for the crazy things we do.

Difference made legal, by the power of majority and then denied the right to vote, leaves the minority with so very little, and certainly no hope.

Sometimes a law is unjust even on its face, and the denying of 1st Amendment rights we find it has no place. I hope that by now you are able to finally see, the distinction between defying the law, and outright anarchy.

There is nothing new about civil disobedience at its very core. There was Shadrach, and Meshach and Abednego and I propose there's more. The Boston Tea Party has also paved the very way, for the civil disobedience that we now use today.

Also lest that you somehow unmindfully forget, that all the laws of Hitler were of the legal sect, and the Hungary Freedom Fighters were illegal in both word and their deeds, just like it used to be illegal to satisfy our Jewish brothers needs.

Lukewarm acceptance of what goes on is more bewildering than outright rejection, while listening to and trying to absorb a moderate white's reflection. Suggesting that one's freedom can somehow surely wait, for some mystical far off season while enduring a sweltering hate.

Injustice is blocking social progress just like a covered ugly boil, an obnoxious negative peace feeding the fire in the South just like oil. Your condemnation of our actions because they precipitate violence from white mobs, sounds just a little like condemning your own employees whenever they get robbed!

One white brother wrote: "*All Christians know that the colored people will receive equal rights in time, but it is possible that you are in too great a religious hurry in your religious minds? It took Christianity almost two thousand years to come this far on the earth.*" My brother please do tell me what do you think your freedom's worth?

Perhaps this brother as well as others suffers a misconception of time, And thinks that **Progress** just happens from the grinding in our minds. Perhaps as an **Extremist** my nonviolent efforts are whacked, and as I stand in the middle of two opposing Negro forces that my own "**somebodiness**" is lacked.

Neither the "**do-nothingism**" of the Negro middle class, nor the hatred of the Black Nationalist, will bless a better way, till the sweet influence of the church ushers Christ love here today! If this nonviolent philosophy had not emerged, by now it is for certain, that we would be mopping blood as it's sopped up by our curtains.

Please recall that an oppressed people cannot remain oppressed forever. The yearning for freedom eventually manifests itself cause the unconscious is too clever, and that is what has happened to the Negro you must see. Cause something has reminded him of his birthright to be free!

But wasn't Lincoln an Extremist, and St Paul and Jesus Christ, And Thomas Jefferson: ***"We hold these truths to be self-evident, that all men are created equal ..."*** as he celebrated life! So you can imagine that an Extremist is not such a bad place to be, Perhaps the South, the nation and the world are in need of creative extremists like me!

I had hoped that the white ***"Middle of the Roader"*** would immediately see the need. Yet I am appreciative of the few that are still willing to march and bleed. There are some exceptions a few just to note, Reverend Stallings, and some Catholic leaders are a few that I can quote.

But despite these notable exceptions, I must honestly reiterate, that I have been disappointed with the way the church deals with HATE. Note that I say this as a preacher of the gospel, who loves the church I'm in; who was nurtured in its bosom; who has preached of **Love** and **Sin**.

When I led the Bus Boycott, I thought we'd somehow find support, but instead the faces of our white brothers found new ways to contort. Some have been outright opponents, refusing to understand, and calling us out of name for the justice we demand.

We must come to see, and realize as the courts have always declared, that it is wrong to say, "Give up your rights" since they may cause another to error. Society must protect the robbed and rightly punish the thief; anything short of this refuses the just man all relief.

One day the South will know as it looks back to recall, that these children of God that sat down, stood up for the best that's in us all. They were standing up for the values and the things we do esteem, it wasn't about the Lunch Counter, it was about the American Dream.

I'm afraid this memo is much too long to take your precious time; I never thought I had these many thoughts to get up off my mind. Please forgive me if anything I've said takes the narrow way, and contorts the streams of truth that we have served here today.

I pray and hope that this letter finds you strong in the ways of Christ, and one day we can sit and meet on the sunny side of life. Someplace where the fog of hate has been dissipated by our duty, so that it gives way to the radiant stars of love and their scintillating beauty.

Yours for the cause ….a simple reprise by Boz

**** I encourage everyone to take the time to read the actual, "Letter From A Birmingham Jail". It will astound, amaze and maybe even bless you.***

A Mission Still To Fulfill

A Mission Still To Fulfill, a journey still to take.
There are places we must go before our history we make,
Tons of purpose, tons of reasons,
and lots of climbing in this season.

A Mission Still To Fulfill, to help our fellow man.
To aid the battered and abused to help them make a stand.
So we volunteer, and give our time to women, kids and men,
Believing that together we can help affect the end.

A Mission Still To Fulfill, and a very long way to go.
There's more than a few bricks and hoses too buried where we hoe.
Not everyone is pulling with us, we see it yet today,
Some would rather let rocks fly than to let us have our way.

A Mission Still To Fulfill, and there's just no time for stoppin.
Though we know there are those that would rather spend this time shoppin.
Tell me what is the value of a single human Life,
And isn't there a cause to now help prevent their strife?

A Mission Still To Fulfill, the civil rights train can't quit.
Not while countless souls are still enslaved and one dear child is hit.
There's a basic worth of people for every Body on this earth,
That we must all sign as one accord whenever there's a birth!

A Mission Still To Fulfill, doing what you must
Even in the face of circumstances that kick up all kinds of dust.
Going from failure on to failure without ever being assuaged,
Taking each new step deep in courage, to press on when you're afraid.

A Mission Still To Fulfill, a work remains to do

And this work can only be complete if I can work with you.
With my hand in your hand and your hand in my hand one day it will be done,
Then we will all bow before the grace that is the sitting Son.

One Man, On Purpose: Rock the Joint

One man that lives on purpose, is a man that lives on **point**.
So God called Dr. King to rock this twisted **joint**.

But why did you do it, I'm now inspired to **ask**? What would make a man walk, such a lonely **path**?

Martin you lived for a purpose, and pursued a Godly **vision**, and because you did, just what God asked, you suffered shame and **derision**.

Purpose is a force that is hard to **contain**, so now there are freedoms and souls like you to **blame**.

Not really just to blame, but more to just to **thank**, and yet there were so many, who would enjoy them all too **late**.

Perhaps there were others who came at an earlier **time**, who chose not to walk on purpose and to God's vision they were **blind**.

Perchance in time there was a woman, a boy or a **girl**, that decided that they couldn't walk their mission, and their sails did not **unfurl**.

Maybe some have decided, to take the road that is **low**, because it seemed plain to them, to be the easy way to **go**.

But A. Langston said if you lose your dreams, then you will **die**, just like a "Broke Winged" bird that now cannot **fly**.

Paul Lawrence said that it would fester, like a raisin in the **sun**, so you better work out your potential, and that goes for **everyone**.

A man that lives his making has a purposed filled burden to **bear**, but the strength of the Spirit will surely get you **there**.

And women too were born, for such a time as **this**. Because truly God already knew Rosa Parks would **exist**.

What then can be said, so that we walk out our grand **design**, But step out of the boat just like Peter, the Spirit says, "The water's **fine**."

One man that lives on purpose, is a man that makes a **point**. So God called Dr. King to rock this twisted **joint**.

The Dream Alive

The Dream is Alive, and I mean still,
They thought we'd give up but we never will.
Havin a dream requires a maintenance plan,
To tweak possibilities, beyond the grasp of man.

The dream is for our children,
to run free while they play.
Without the worry of ole Jim Crowe,
Cause we're in a different day.

The dream sets free our imagination,
and breaks the shackles of our souls.
And grants us new lenses to view our world,
Not those rose colored ones, but gold.

To some the dream is still surreal,
Even as it becomes our fact.
Just remember from whence you come,
Cause there ain't no turning back.

Envision witnesses from our past as they see the President,
As they look down and see the scene they wonder where time went.
And I can sense some satisfaction, and it's not just among the blacks.
A Dream is coming to this land as we straighten up our backs.

Cause on many backs were borne the weight,
of carrying America into the Dream.
Just like the shoulders that laid the tracks,
Of the steel monster that blew steam.

I still can see Dr King's face,
as he looks past me to tomorrow.
Don't dare think the struggle over son,

Or you'll wake one day to sorrow.

The Dream is Alive, and I mean still,
They said we'd give up but I never will.
The dream is my personal plan,
To tweak my reach, beyond the grasp of man.

The Bitter Cup For Freedom

He hath shewed thee, O man, what is good; and what doth the LORD require of thee, but to do justly, and to love mercy, and to walk humbly with thy God? **Micah 6:8**

I hear the Lord saying, There is one thing that I require of thee.
Not to just go on a walk, but to go there as free!

And "Go There" he went and not a minute too late,
His willingness to go, went in spite of the hate.

In fact he went there in love, unrestrained by the spite,
He walked as if he were following an off world, great light!

To some his walk was a Waltz, as if he were proud,
To others his walk was a March, because he went un-allowed.

They say that, God's Mercies are new every day,
And surely they are what guided him to walk a straight way.

Martin walked with intention as he blazed a new trail,
And then showed others the walk, and said it couldn't fail.

A Just man accentuates the justice that he can see,
But it may not prove obvious to those that bind liberty.

See Liberty unlike Justice is never pictured blind.
But she is offered to all that our open shores can find.

Nelson Mandela: Good Bye Our Hero[4]

Come quick, come tell me how do you do, How do you say it to a man that was true.

He's more than a champion for what he endured, Mutual destruction was almost self assured.

Johannesburg & Cape Town seemed like worlds away, Yet for all that they went through we'll visit there today.

All for a man, with a vision for simple equality, Yet denied just for having skin, the same as those like me.

South Africa, Transkei, and the march to human freedom, ANC and apartness come see the Spear Of The Nation.

Apartheid was the issue and with your life you drove it home, The Long Walk To Freedom &Robben Island shows your walk was not alone.

How do you say good bye to a hero? When it seems he's conquered all, For 27 years he suffered captors, yet while you stumble, you never fall.

Rolihlahla was the name given, Trouble maker is its root,
Nelson is what we call you now, You are a hero now to boot.

Xhosa tribe raised by a king, Thembu clan by rights a chieftain, Rebel then prisoner be, your law degree would only grief them.
Policemen beat ole Biko down, struggle on dear children of the war, Charged with treason for seeking rights, we've seen this play unfold before.

A dozen tipping points all around, Sharpeville massacre is not the least, Afrikaners think they'll lock it down but the news portray they act like beasts.

From Gandhi on to Dr. King, Mr. Lincoln, and on to Churchill. You study and apply it all and never turn back but know that they will.

Winne, de Klerk, and then I add the honorable Bishop Tutu, Just a few names that interlock the work and life changes that you do.

How do you say good bye to a hero?, Who has done more for the world than superman, Thank you and blessings for your upright hand and for all the changes you have ushered!

7. A Sign For The Nation

Exodus 4:8 And it shall come to pass, if they will not believe thee, neither hearken to the voice of the first sign, that they will believe the voice of the latter sign.

Sign, a token; indication.

The Lord has given us a sign of His presence. In fact there are several of these signs. Some of these signs fall under the heading of ***General***. There are others that can be considered ***Special Signs*** of His presence or handiwork. This group of poems points to both of the types of His presence.

If you do not think that you can say conclusively that you detect His presence. God and His desire can still be impressed by how we treat one another. These poems reflect that a certain moral character toward your brother and sister is in order. And that turpitude is wrong and punishable.

The Strength of a Man

Mayor Fred L. Armstrong, what can I say?
What would make a man give in this humble way?
After serving on City Council and even the Columbus police,
What would make you give more and not just give the least?

After trips to maybe India, China and others in the far East,
Why didn't Kathy just tell you to chill out, stop, and to cease?
Why didn't Gretchen or maybe even Shannon,
Just pull out your old police cuffs and decide to teach you a lesson?

But the fact that they didn't is a testament to,
To the serving that goes on in a house that is lead by you.
You have improved through the city and revitalized the town
You had served four full terms before you thought to just sit down.

There's the National Road and still other road projects completed,
There's the several new building efforts oft now being repeated.
This corner and that corner around town, you should all take a look,
Soon we'll be found on the cover of someone's brand new book.

You've charmed business people and made them pay the price,
For thinking Columbus was too small or maybe just too nice.
From Sport Tourism Programs or Foundation For Youth growth
It's clear that while you didn't lead these efforts that you still support them both.
My manager constantly reminds me of this as his leadership role,

To remove the barriers that will impede your productive people's souls.
The things that will prevent their wings from stretching out to fly,
Are the same things that if neglected will poke you in the eye.

So while we appreciate that you have not run and done it all,
We know that you stacked up the boxes that made them all stand tall.
So we thank you for your work and also for your leadership.
We appreciate that during the flood that you didn't abandon ship.
I thank you for working with City Council and your helping them to stand up tall,
We thank you for the cities transformation that we expect to reach us one & all.
We especially appreciate the time borrowed from your lovely little granddaughters.
Now stand up take a bow and go enjoy Josie, Ellie, Amelia, and Harper.

Ready For More

Premise: It's Possible, It's Worth It, it's Hard, and ...It's Done!

Ready for more, of what's now in store,
It's Possible is what we once said.
With all hands on deck, we turned the tide.
We got 'er done, with an engine painted Red!

Ready for more. No it's not a bore.
The Possible has become the fact!
BHP of over 4755, and excess power to spare,
"*This genset has that imperceptible Knack*"!

We're ready for more, once the Alphas hit the shore,
It's Worth it! is the charge from the helm.
Hedgehog is the future, more power to the field.
We are building a new Cummins Realm!

Ready for more, Proton Plus ratings score.
It's Worth it! Our dollars per kilowatt: Density: power.
This diesel genset stands to break records.
Just watch as Field Test racks up the hours.

Ready for more, no waiting on seats sore.
***It's* Hard**, says the press and customer too!
They raised the bar and we delivered,
But there is more that we have now to do.

Ready for more, of what customer's pay for.
It's Hard, to give people just what they ask.
Things break and fail in the background.
Sometimes the 7 Steps are a thankless task!

Ready for more, of what reporters adore!
***It's* Done**, yet production seems so far away.
M3 is off in the distance, M5 is off too.
But a Beta/Market Seed might be sold today!

Cummins, Ready for more,
They'll say you did it before!
It's Done, once the C3500 is delivered.
This huge diesel product will pave the way,
But when V20 and Gas comes then they'll shiver!

Black History Month

Black History Month…it just doesn't sound right
How a nation that values us could only give us a few nights,
To instill some positives into the air,
When there's so much negative wafting out there,
To combat profiling we would listen to King,
When Justice is suggested Medgar Evers we would bring,
What can you do to instill harmony?
Remind your soul that today it is **free!**

Diaspora

Diaspora: The dispersion or scattering of people with common origin, background or beliefs.
They say we are all from one man Adam, they say that the Jews have come from all over to return to Israel, they say that African & Americans… Question: What do you call Diaspora?

Get it together Diaspora; you are brought together for a reason,
You've been apart but you're together now, yet it's only for a season.

Get it together mighty men of valor, both the youthful and the wise,
You've looked at the world too differently, try now to see eye to eye.

Come together mighty Nubian queens, and my sultry princess of the night sky.
She's your mother, sister, and auntie too, so shun words that make the other cry.

Come together young Ghana prince join hands, stand up2 and be accounted.
Lay down the gun, that's enough lip son, now your words must move this mountain.

Many have done virtuously, but will you heed the beck of unity and answer to its call?
Or will you continue to stare and slander me, and anticipate my reckonings fall.

Come together mighty European and wise men of the East
Your blood is not superior and certainly not the least

Bind your hearts you Native sons and sons of Judah too
Reel on in your checkered past your **Purpose** has need of you

All hands on deck and shoulders too we have progress now to make
For we're in this thing all as one or know ye not what's at stake?

True enough there's a challenge laying up ahead for all of us that matter.
Recall the Dream, lay down the scheme, lets coalesce, bind, and not scatter.

But there's more than one way to get the job done and where there's a will there's a way!
But it's for certain that we won't get er done, if we put off till later what needs doin today!

Black Renaissance

Black I am by de-man,
Whether or not it's popular they judge my hand.
They dare not look to what's in the mind,
For another "Renaissance Man" they may find.
They see my knuckles and they get scared,
cause they can smell the nap and kink O' my hair.
They can hear my stride 'cause my march is tight,
But they are profiling my actions, and that's not right.
Check out my stance and see that it's wide,
Cause there's more to the man than what you see outside.
I heard King say that he's lookin for the day,
"When the character of a man", is what makes his way,
But all these exceptions to their rules keep emergin,
While the people at large continue their sufferin.
Obama, Rice, and Winfrey are some,
But if the guard would drop low, more would come,
I'd like to be an exception to the rule,
but it's no self proclaimed title and I'm no fool.
So for now I see that the bars set high,
So I'll keep doin my thing till the day I die.
Just let me do mine and I'll make a way for more.
A better day is what I knows in store.
Black by demand is what they say,
But my content screams, "I'm more today!"

The Challenge of Reconciliation in the 21st Century

Challenge: To summon to action or effort. To stimulate i.e. **Challenging**: Calling for full use of one's abilities or resources.

Reconcile: To reestablish a close relationship between.

The Challenge of Reconciliation

Reconciling the minds of many often comes only at great price.
By example reconciling the soul of Man, costs our Savior His life.
Reconciliation of a nation will neither come at great ease, But to ignore this crucial requirement may surely bring progress to its knees.
The challenge here is thus far, more than "dimpled chads" have been thrown away, But also those lives invested in a system, that never counted them once that day.
"Well, let's not cry over spilled milk", is what I hear many say. "Let's forget the past and live in the present, that's a much more excellent way".
But those that ignore the mistakes of the past, are doomed in the present you see, There's much to be said for history's cycles, but not much for problems redundancy.
To good Dr. Martin reconciliation means; dispatching "the sweltering heat of oppression" Reestablishing right relations with leaders, caught in "interposition and nullification".
And so my friends before us lies the 1st challenge of the 21st Century. One achieved only through prayer and struggle - The Hope of True Unity.
A "Challenge" in the orient it's said is, "A Dangerous Opportunity". The question you may ask, "Is it worth the risk?" Well certainly if you're asking me.
Any physician knows his credo says upfront, "Do no harm", But to heal a land we must go man to man, and not pacify with charm.
A whole millennium stands before us, to unite or rift apart, Extend your hand and heal a man, communication is where it starts.

An Island or A Nation

9-11 a day that we should remember. In the shadows of my mind I still see the burning embers.

Pillars of tall clouds and rising toxic smoke, fall like a haze and cover the running city folk.

Am I an Island? Or does this scene still touch me. Am I truly a part of this Great Land called Liberty?

Katrina has struck and the Images come in like waves. First there's the shock, then the awe, then finally daring roof top saves.

Didn't you have family there? Better check your next of kin. Have you seen the weather report, a new storm is coming in?

Or is a man an Island? Are these actions affecting me? Do I have the slightest clue about Christianity?

The neighbors lost some loved ones down in New Orleans today. The water crashed the broken dikes, and may never recede they say.

Mississippi, Alabama, and Louisiana too. Thousands of displaced citizens, what will America do?

No man can be an Island! What hurts you must hurt me. If babies are hungry and without clothes, how dare I say, "But they're free".
In my picture of America what displaces you, must displace me. But there's one solution that rings from the heart, "Let our giving spread Liberty!"

For the Survivors of Hurricane Katrina, and All Americans

We Need To Pray:

Just some thoughts on the power of this day.
Why would we waste this opportunity to pray.
He's always there listening, for the time He's your choice.
If I'm anything like Him then He enjoys hearing His child's voice.

Sharing just a few insights on the pace of the day.
Don't dare waste that small opportunity to pray,
and share with the Creator our most basic of needs.
When He has been so good in spite of all of our deeds,

He gives us food to eat and a warm place to stay.
Why waste another opportunity to simply kneel down and pray.

8. Glory From A Star

Numbers 14:21 But as truly as I live, all the earth shall be filled with the glory of the LORD.

Glory: adoring praise or worshipful thanksgiving: Give glory to God.

The picture above is one of my wife Charlene. This next list of poems I first thought to keep hidden and private. I decided against that because while Charlene is my wife whom I hold dear. She is in many ways my muse. She ignites a passion in me that I believe many people look for in poetry. God truly blessed me.

I likewise must admit to the pet names that she and I have for one another since without knowing them you may miss a bit of one or two poem's flair. I call her "Candy Girl", since when I met her she was working at the "candy counter" of the University of Dayton Student Union. I always joke that I came away with the sweetest treat there. I also call her "Star"of this David. She in turn calls me, "The Light".

One piece that I am especially proud of is my song, "You're The Key". Maybe one day you will have a chance to hear it. However, as in every life it is not just "peaches and cream". To appreciate this reality take a read of the glory expressed in "Bliss".

Anniversary Roses

Roses are red, violets are lovely,
Maximum swerve comes from the bubbly.

The drink we serve is just sparkling grape,
Trying to ensure we can walk the tape.

Passionate kisses from my queen bee.
Maximum hugs are returned by me.

Twenty seven year anniversary of our love.
Ordained and sanctified by the Father above,

Blessing our walk with power and peace.
Heavenly rain causing all strife to cease.

Swept up in the care we have for each other.
Assured we could never find this love with another.

Anniversary

A man and his wife, I knew from the start that you were to be
the owner of my heart.
The house on Stewart St in which I first lived gave subtle
indication whose love was to give.
Wonderfully delicious, skin fair and smooth I could eat up
your kisses when I'm short on food.
A heaven sent beauty who prays for my health, I'm devoted to
you so I'll gladly share all my wealth.
The doctor who spanked you, first birthed me, God knew then
whose wife you were to be.
A Sigma's Sweetheart and a dancer too, you knew I couldn't
keep my heart off of you.
The phone calls, the dances, the time spent alone, all served to
assure me I'd make you my own.
The years past, the children, the house made a home these are
the reasons you sit on my throne.
Candy Girl, Star, Mighty Ethiopian Queen, my first and last
love I call you Charlene!

Bliss

Day 1
I awake you with the softest of kiss, and consider the state I now call "Wedded Bliss".
You stir, "Why would you kiss me while I'm tryin ta sleep?"
"Have you prayed the Lord your soul to keep?"

Day2
Today is the second and I knew from the start, that you and the covers would not soon part.
"Me get up early, are you crazy, No- way ", "You know I always sleep late on Saturday!"

Day 3
Today is a Sunday, so I let you sleep in, I'd 'try to wake you up but we both know who'd win.
Before I leave for class you are up and about, ...but I think it's just so you can lock me out.

Celestial

You are my Black Star, more precious by, far than anyone's
Diamonds or Pearls.
And your value to me exceeds your capacity to act like the rest
of the girls.

Yes you're worth more demanding than emeralds, with more
class
than a tear drop of Jade.
But like the timelessness of that lone tear drop, your beauty to
me
will never fade.

Because your poise is more refined than Zirconium and the
fire in your eyes a Star Sapphire.
Which leads me to say in a most convincing way that you are
my one true desire.

Yes, I've paid the price of your ruby lips, and the cost to touch
Topaz skin.
And though I have paid it for nineteen years or more now, I
would gladly pay it again.

Cause an Onyx of your expense is undervalued, and
Aquamarine at your cost is well spent.
My, dear Star you must see you're worth it to me because a
love
like ours is heaven sent.

So I could not trade you for Bloodstone, Amethyst, or the
rarest of Opals.
Dear Ebonite you see though you give your love free I
recognize that you are Celestial.

My Queen

All my love to you Charlene, my mighty Ethiopian Queen, heaven must have sent you down from Stardust Magazine.

You see you have rocked my lonely world, my one and only girl, since that 1st day that you said you'd stay and give our love a whirl.

But today I am blinded, at first I didn't mind it, I thought you needed a push so then I just stepped behind it.

But to my huge surprise, you left the other guys, and now it's me that you love and I can't believe my eyes!

So it's true what they say when we don't get our way, that we often sit and pout because of the games that people play!

So that's never been our game, we have always stayed the same, except for lovin each other more, and more, cause that's our claim to fame.

Yes it's almost turned to dawn, and while time is almost gone, you don't have to worry about me my Queen, cause I'll keep holdin on!

Holding on to your hand, cause I got a better plan, to blow up all my purpose girl, I think you understand.

But your look says you don't know, how I intend to grow, and be larger in my destiny once God gets me in my flow.

So let's focus now on you, and the crazy things you do, just to keep our love alive my girl or should I call you Boo?

The Star of David is who you are, and though I travel far, it's you I always think about when I get in a car.

Cause I imagine you beside, as I step into my ride, My Queen with me on God's green Earth, because my Queen she is my guide.

So I'll bring this to an end, so I don't step off in sin, yes we'll close it down for now my love till you start me up again!

To My Mighty Ethiopian Queen

Just Stay

Over 8 years ago I asked you to stay, and somehow or another you found a way.

To stick around with me and share in my life, and to give me two children after becoming my wife.

I can't tell the future but I'll find a way to love you forever if you would just stay!

We've had our ups, and we've had our downs, but my days are much brighter when my Star is around.

I'm not getting younger, but I'll find a way to cherish your innocence if you would just stay.

From Indy to the Nati and to Indy again, when I had first moved there you were more than my friend.

We've been to Hawaii and stopped in L.A., but I'll show you the world if you would just stay.

Let's Go! Star

Let's Go! Star,
To some place far away, someplace alone.
Somewhere not near, yet someplace like home.

To someplace familiar, and oddly reminiscent,
Somewhere we've heard about, and desired to visit.

To someplace they speak English, so we'd know what to say,
Like when they say, Hello, we'd say, "Have a nice day!"

I don't want to be known there so I can fit right in,
But I don't want to be odd there, like a man with 3 chins.

To someplace that won't take much money, to get there and back,
Somewhere they won't mind that your skin is beautifully black.

To somewhere closer than yonder, and without a layover gate,
Somewhere we can get to and not stay up too late.

If I told you that your favorite place is the place we will go,
Could I get you to go there and we leave all this snow!

Can we pack it up tomorrow and then leave here by nine?
If so you have my attention, and I will follow you blind.

My Love

You've given your hand, you've given your heart, and one day you'll give me the rest.
I've given my love all sorts of fine and exquisite things but one day I'll give her the best.

So today my Queen how long has it been, 20 years and yet there's much more inside me.
That I'll gladly give just to my love if your ruby warm kisses occasionally imbibe me.

Yes, your kisses they are like honeydroplets that steam like the dew on warm earth,
And your soft caress of my neck always makes me a wreck as I now fantasi of rebirth.

In my glistened age I cherish hand holding, and just slow hugging my love on the couch.
And though it may be the height of simplicity just touching your cheek makes me say ouch.

Yes my Star I can go on for much, much, longer for it's your love that gives me the strength.
I'm not just an average young man, when I'm within your hands my powers extend to the "N^{th}".

For your love my love would surely stand-up and be more than alone I could be.
But I need you to know that as in love we grow, your love must take all of me.

A HEART, A BOX, A KEY, AND A LOCK

A Heart, a box, a Key, and a lock
If your love were a closed door I'd just have to Knock.
A Heart, a box, a Key, and a lock

A Heart, a box, a lock, and a Key
If not for your love where would I be?
In this marriage I'm free to be me.
A Heart, a box, a lock, and a Key

A Key, a box, a lock, and a Heart
To look back is to know that '86 came since the start.
A Key, a box, a lock, and a Heart

A Heart, a lock, a key, and a box,
For 22 years now we've leaned on the Rock.
And you've held it together with,
A Heart, a lock, a key, and a box

A HEART, that holds deeply to both family and friends, that loves from its core not wanting to end.

A BOX, to protect belongings, both big and the small, the box enlarges to contain one and all.

A KEY, to gain access, with just a smile or a wink. Flashing soft hazel eyes that change in a blink.

AND A LOCK, to shut out the harshness around knowing that safe in our love, true peace can be found.

And so in this package I think can be found, the symbol of a circle that keeps going around. This endless pattern represents Eternity, which is how long I'll keep, loving on Charlene "Star" Bosley.

TILL THE LIGHT GOES OUT

You may oft wonder when will our life get right, when
regardless of planning our cash gets tight.
Then you look at the bills and your hearts filled with doubt.
But, I'll always love you till the Light goes out.

When the kids get lost caught up in play, and your searching
for them makes a wreck of your day.
And there comes the time that you can't help but shout.
Know that I'll always love you till the Light goes out.

Even when both of the cars seem to give up the ghost, just at a
time that we needed them most.
When the challenges of the day you can not surmount.
Believe that I'll always love you till the Light goes out;

So when Regis and Kathy can't be seen on TV, and the
regularly scheduled programs all end up "Soap" free.
Don't turn to Oprah to see what she's about,
Cause it's then that I'll love you till the Light goes out.

If our trips here and there start to "Stress Out" your mind. And
you try remaining calm but no peace you can find.
Even if I disappoint you and in sadness you pout.
I'll always love you till the Light goes out.

You may ask if I love you still. My reply is that I always will.
Take your burdens to the Lord cause I know he has clout,
and remember I will always love YOU till the "Light" goes
Out.

9. The Look We Love To See

Matthew 11:3 And said unto him, Art thou he that should come, or do we <u>look</u> for another?

Look: the way in which a person or thing appears to the eye or to the mind; aspect: He has the look of an honest man.

God says that nothing can separate us from His love. Because of this if we look hard and sincerely enough we can see him in some of the most unexpected places. If we look hard enough and sincerely enough we can see His love in our brothers and our sisters.

If you have a spiritual eye for Him you may even recognize His blessings of love in your friends and family. You may look and find His love in your community or on the job. The challenging piece to this is that you have to look for it. Sometimes we never find the love that was right in front of us, only because we failed to look.

My great friends the Jacksons and the Woods have found a great love because they made it a point to look.

I recall that there used to be a popular song, "***The Look of Love.***"[6] I fondly recall that Look of Love when I looked over pictures of my Mom. That is one under the chapter heading. I believe that she is holding Tim. We lived on Dempsey St, at the time. I also had that look when my daughter was born. Take a look around, you may be lucky enough to be closer to love than you thought, just look.

Daddy's Gemstone

This Gemstone my dear is presented your 16th year because your
birth to us was quite glorious.
And it's yours you see if you can stay drug free and never with
the police become "Notorious".

Yes real Diamonds are rare, like the curl of your hair, and are
meant to set your eyes on fire.
Just remain true to me until someone's bride you will be and
don't dare to my face be a liar.

So the Ruby is **Hot Red** and you know that it is said that it,
"Sets Fire to the Heart's Passion".
Just let the boys all please know, that they must stand in a row,
but your kisses have all been rationed.

My daughter you are blessed, and we pray for you, "God's Best",
just be sure you give it back to Him.
Cause if you can't thank Him for your care, like the "**Buck**" clothes
you wear, your future will begin to look slim.

Just know that you have our love along with the Spirit from
above, so there is nothing in this world that can stop you.
So bless the Lord with your voice and always make Him your first
choice, and then even the enemy cannot block you.

Starlet of this David, though we had these thoughts, we saved it,
and it was set aside until maturity.
So like the poem written goes, that true love always grows, and if
you truly love someone set them free.
Christen you are our Gemstone.

This Rose Is a Pledge

With this rose I do decree,
That you will always feel love from me.

This is my promise and this is my vow,
I'll love you then like I love you now.

With this rose I promise a tomorrow,
And commit that I'll stay in joy or in sorrow.

But even in love sometimes things will go south,
And I have to repent for the things in my mouth.

But with this rose I assure you my heart,
So I reserve it for you, some light in the dark.

I promise you love like Christ loves the church,
And that's why I will always place your heart first.

You Are Precious

You are precious in His sight, a precious ointment of pure delight.
A precious stone true and rare, with long silky locks or kinky hair.
He glories in your precious fruit, with a sassy "tude" and passion to boot.
The Word says, more precious than of gold, your stock goes up, and never gets old.
What makes you so is precious blood, whose spirit flows in like a flood.
In the image of precious Jesus Christ, now full of his precious life.
Just trust him with your precious faith, cause in his arms you should feel safe.
His precious promises say it is yours, cause it's your heart he does adore.
His precious city will welcome you in, all because you've been born again.
You are precious.

10. Many Appearances, One Name

Numbers 9:16 So it was alway: the cloud covered it by day, and the appearance of fire by night.

Appearance: the state, condition, manner, or style in which a person or object appears; outward look or aspect: a table of antique appearance; a man of noble appearance.

The picture represents what the chapter heading says. My brothers and I are many appearances of that one name Bosley. There is Marty, Tommy, Tim and myself, Bosley's all.

In many regards my poems attempt to capture the note referenced to the appearance of fire at night. I have told many people that I believe that the Lord often wakes me in the small hours of the night so that He will have my undivided attention. I say the appearance of fire since many times my words bring out a passion and sense of fiery emotion that may catch some folk off guard. In most cases I can't take credit for it. I give the Lord full credit. Many times it is as though I am just listening in on the conversation of angels.

Just like both the cloud and the pillar of fire operated to lead Israel while in the wilderness, yet it was the same God that led them. Here I share several poems written, some prophetically, and some concerning different churches. I like to think we are each serving God as best we know how. I truly believe that each and every House of God is Holy Ground.

Drawing by: Al Martin

The Calvary Crusader

The Calvary Crusader is a soldier for Christ. Marching into
war he would gladly give his life.
But his Savior shed His blood for all just to make them free, so
the battles that we face in life are a part of Destiny.
We wear the armor of our Lord, our feet covered in His peace.
We study to show ourselves approved of God, the greatest
must be the least.
For we are servants one and all, we do our masters will. All
must rise to meet the call, come from Golgotha's Hill.
"To spread the gospel far and wide!", is our battle cry. Until
that trumpet sounds above and we meet Jesus in the sky!

Dayspring Motto:

Summer, Fall, Winter, Spring,
God's already doing a brand new thing.

He's not bound by time, He moves in seasons.
The love of Christ is the only reason.

I have faith that this brand new thing will bless my spirit
while I'm here at Dayspring.

For the city of Columbus it's a brand new day, sin is exposed
by the Dayspring's rays.

But the love of Jesus gives us life anew, washed in his Spirit
through and through.

For the persecuted, the poor, those in pain, and the dying, the
tears wiped away there'll be no more crying.

We live a life abundantly, because in Christ Jesus there's
Liberty.

My mind is focused on what my Lord will bring, cause I've
found a home here at Dayspring!

Faith Hope and Love

Faith Hope and then comes Love
Three virtues worth us speaking of

Faith comes by hearing that there's a reason to be,
In strong belief of Jesus Christ as the Savior you see.

It is the substance and stuff that made the Universe.
What's more is it's created everything on the Earth.

Without Works it is dead this we must note,
Cause it's the thing that made Noah build a big boat.

Then comes Hope to this blessed mix that we have.
That's Bible Belief not a vain wish about things we might grab.

In most cases it deals with our expected end,
To one day live in Heaven with Jesus our friend.

Because this is just like a true guarantee,
That our Hope will be fulfilled when He shouts Come Hither to me!

Now Love is a virtue we are commanded to show.
And when we've had enough there's more we must grow.

We must willingly give it to our sister and brother,
Just to blow the world's mind showing Love for one another.

Then we heap it like hot coals on those that show hate,
To win them to Christ to help us celebrate.

Faith Hope and Love a fine mix of 3,
Established in the heavens to set this world free!

Gospel Extravaganza

Jesus' disciples sung a hymn when they left communion for the Olivet Mount,
Back in the day, Peter and his brothers knew what good gospel was about!
Today some sing the melody, yet to sing with the Spirit is rare,
To be set ablaze by a songs sweet lyrics truly sends a crackle into the air

A religious song, poem or melody of God and all of His glorious ways,
Is a tune I love to carry in my pocket so that I'm prepared for sadder days,
Good days it's in your pocket, so on the bad days you can move it to the heart
So that even in sorrow you enjoy the **Son's** rays, and to him know you are a part

Ephesians 5 guides us to speak psalms, hymns and even spiritual songs!
Singing and making melody for the Lord; because to Him you do really belong.
So we lift up our voice in Praise and bless the Lord for each granted day,
And if a trial is our portion, we praise more fervently because we know He'll make a way!

Then Colossians 3 tells us, To let the word of Christ dwell in each of you richly
This can happen only in Christ because where he is there is true Liberty
Admonishing wisdom; teaching and in psalms and hymns and spiritual singing,
Walking with grace in your hearts to the Lord, because to him daily we're clinging.

John's Book of Revelation, 5:8 picks up what others may have dropped,
And tells of the one that opened the Book when we thought all heaven had stopped.
And they sung a new song, saying, "You're worthy to take the **Book**, and to open the **Seals**",
Through his death, burial and resurrection, he's redeemed us by his blood and made an appeal.
An appeal that reaches every kindred, and tongue, and people, and even every nation;
And made us unto our God, kings and priests: and made us rulers of every generation.

So today we present the God News of Christ and share it's redeeming message in song,
And if the tune get's to you please clap your hands, stamp your feet or just plan to sing along.
Cause the God that we serve is best worshipped with surrendering hands lifted high
And with a rousing chorus of melody, we can lift his praise upward to the sky!

Standing On Holy Ground

Wherever we are in Christ is Holy Ground. God sent His Tabernacle to us to enjoy His Presence, without His presence we get lonely and feel separated from Him. He no longer dwells in temples made with man's hands.

God desires relationship with the man and woman He has made.
But its fear and sin that makes us run ashamed and afraid.
If we would stand and bow our head, we'd know that we have found.
The awesomeness of His presence that we call Holy Ground.
Jacob found His presence one starry night, at Luz it's been said.
When he saw dreams of the Lord above, an image in his Head.
He changed the name to Bethel when he saw angels going up and down.
Then he left a pillar to remember that this place was Holy Ground.
Moses saw a burning bush that could not be diminished.
After tending sheep in Horeb when he thought his life was finished.
He turned aside to see more better this sight that he had seen.
And then heard from the voice of God in a tone that wasn't mean.
Don't come even one step closer, take those shoes now off your feet.
It is the God of Abraham, of Isaac, and of Jacob you must meet.
But before you move another inch there's some truth I must lay down.
The wondrous sight you've seen and the place you stand is Holy Ground.
Sacred, and even dedicated, anointed, and even holy,
Just says that it is set apart for God's uses and that only.

Joshua had an awesome encounter also you must know,
He saw a captain on the field before he took down Jericho.
He asked are you for us or against us, he said, "Nay but for the Lord."
Then he said, "Take off your shoes, because I know you've seen my sword."
The thing that we must recognize is these aren't little plots of holy land.
With some heaven sent reminders of the spots that God commands.
No the Psalmist says, "The earth is the LORD'S, and they that dwell therein."
So we too can be a holy temple once we've been cleansed of sin.
So the relationship God longs for has now come back around.
As we relish in His Presence we can bask on Holy Ground.

Apostolic Church

To the glorious saints of Jerusalem Temple Apostolic Church, We see a host of families here, and Of course God made families first.

He made a host of families, but remember God just started out with two. Yet there are times when your heart looks down when you think, "We're just a few!"

Let not your heart be troubled cause the Lord has got your back, And if you take one step, He'll take two, and will always pick up your slack.

God made a host of families, but He started with just Adam and then Eve. Then He saw the families here needed a pastor that would challenge their power to believe.

So The Lord fashioned a shepherd, and gave him experiences and plenty of heart, And gave him an abundance of wisdom too to keep the lambs and wolves apart.

Then God gave him energy, so that he could run with a pace to see the very end, And then gave him the Holy Ghost with power y'all so that more souls he could win.

Finally a lovely first lady was given to balance out his power, To pick up his spirit when it's down, and to sweeten him when he's sour.

So Bishop Derek Jefferson, you are a blessed man there is no doubt. Whenever there is trouble call on Jesus cause he's the one with clout.

And whenever that you need a friend you know you can call on me. And Dayspring Church will be a help, Love, signed Pastor David C. Bosley.

Lord, We Praise You

We bow our heads to you dear Lord, to you we give all of our praise

We genuflect and give up the yadah and worship you all of our days!

We bow our heads to you dear Lord, to you we surrender our ways.

You've been with us since the beginning of time and it's your love that has ended our daze!

We reverence you Lord we surrender our hearts, to you we raise up our hands.

We accept no idol substitutes from the carnal mind of man.

The Prince of Peace, the Great I am, you alone our God will be.

The half of your glory has never been told but it's to you that we will bend our knee.

And while we bow we lift you up to you we yield all our praise,

And worship to we bring now to you, for you have transformed our ways.

We bow our knees to you dear Lord and it's you we glorify.

We humbly submit to our Father's will till we meet you in the sky!

Thy Kingdom Come Today

Thy Kingdom Come, Thy Will Be Done,
A prophetic prayer for everyone.
Thy Kingdom Come, Thy Will Be Done,
A prayer for God's will on you His son

Thy Kingdom Come, a simple and delightful 3 point phrase,
Said to entreat the Lord and all of His glorious ways.
Thy Will Be Done, right here, right now, down here on this earth.
Right here, right now, a day of blessing in the land of your spirit's birth.

Thy Kingdom Come, Thy Will Be Done,
A prophetic move for everyone.
Thy Kingdom Come, Thy Will Be Done,
A house of prayer for all who come.

Emphasized and stressed as more of a praise,
Said to increase you and yours for all of your days.
A model prayer spoken out loud just for Heaven to now bless.
A way for our soul, to say to our spirit an undivided, "Yes!"

Thy Kingdom Come, do it Lord as we take thy holy bread,
Knowing that it's from the spirit we need to eat, whenever we are fed.
Thy Will Be Done, as we make up our mind to love on the debtor,
As we slay the flesh in order to forgive and to accept your Word by the letter.

Thy Kingdom Come, as you lead us from temptation it is said,
Thy Will Be Done, as you deliver us from the evil in our head!

For thine is the kingdom, and the power, and the glory yet today.
And it will not change until your Kingdom comes and shows us a better Way!

Thy Kingdom Come, Thy Will Be Done,
A prophetic house for daughters and for sons.
Thy Kingdom Come, Thy Will Be Done,
A God ordained ministry to bless everyone.

The Word Is The Key

I hold the key,
that sets me free.
The Word controls my destiny.
Yield to the Word,
and you to will see…
that Jesus gives life MORE abundantly.

11. Jesus, In A Vision, Salvation

Proverbs 29:18 Where there is no vision, the people perish: but he that keepeth the law, happy is he.

Vision: a vivid, imaginative conception or anticipation: ***visions of wealth and glory.***

The transliterated name of Jesus means salvation. As such when we call him we are calling for salvation, a deliverer, or our savior. This in turn causes me to believe that without him my life will be full of problems. The scriptures say in John10:10 ***The thief cometh not, but for to steal, and to kill, and to destroy: I am come that they might have life, and that they might have it more abundantly.*** With Jesus we have an abundant life.

The synonym for this chapter is ***vision***. I believe that we can, with little argument tie Jesus to that ***vision***. So I would say in response to the salvation that is found in Jesus that ultimately, where there is no Jesus, the people perish. Sometimes we say it like this, "No Jesus, No Peace! Know

Jesus, Know Peace." I even think that this saying is appropriate here: "Seven days without Jesus makes one weak!"

The picture is a photograph of Dad in the Army. After high school like so many he joined the Army. I'm certain he had plans and visions for his life ahead. Many are the plans of a man's heart, but ***only God knows***. That is something we say frequently at Dayspring..."O.G.K."! That doesn't say that you do not make a plan, or catch a vision. However, in the final analysis you have to make it ok, OGK.

Why Jesus

Why Jesus, some may ask do I call you Adonai,
He is love sent from heaven would be my lone reply,
Why wonderful counselor?
Another query from the crowd it comes,
Because Parakletosis the title reserved for God's only son,
Because in the court room we need a Paraclete to get the tough jobs done.

A Street Of Palms

One day the king arrived and rode a street of palms,
One day the adversary laughed at the colt he rode upon

One day he rode in celebration as the crowd cheered out his name,
One day afterward he carried a cross, while enduring agony and pain.

One day the people cried out, "Hosanna", to my Lord,
One day they turned their backs, as if they all were bored.

One day my Savior came to save the sinner and the lost,
One day his blood was shed upon the station of the cross.

One day he hung his head and then gave up the Ghost,
One day he did all this and more, because he loved the most.

One day he bore great infamy just to make us free,
One day he earned us all the right to live in Liberty.

One day soon he will return and it will not be the same.
One day he'll ride in on a horse and his thigh will bear his name!

Creative Faith

If there is a need, plant a spoken seed.
And by faith it will grow, in your spirit you should know.
Though it sounds a bit absurd, that is God's holy word.
If there's a glimmer of desire, throw some seed on that fire.
The words of your mouth, and the meditation of your heart,
will give the seed a proper place to start.
And it will grow to whatever you have to say, that is God's holy way.

A Reason To Hope

A reason was seen in her walk now tall.
A choice given to one and all.

A blessing of purpose now at hand.
To every child, woman, and man.

Potential was granted in this life to express,
Work the Master Key, demonstrated in the press.

Yield to His hand even when the body says, nope.
And know that yet for today we still have Hope.

Cross To Bare

FOXES HAVE HOLES, AND BIRDS HAVE NESTS,

But there is no place found, for the Son of Man to rest.

But on a tree they hung him wide, in his 33rd year he found his stride.

The rugged CROSS of guilt and shame, the chosen place to frame his name.

King of the Jews and of every man, sacrificial lamb sent to finish God's plan.

A plan established by the Blood of One, Known by many as God's own Son.

Faith

Although it has been said that, "faith without works is dead".

There remain many that say, "It's for you that I pray."

Though they may have in their hands, a means to aid this man.

Yet still in their prosperity, they maintain no active charity.

Tell me is this right, in God's Omniscient sight.

No, it's wrong, and I must say that, there is a better way!

Faith and works is real, when it's the Holy Ghost that you feel.

My Gift I Bring

Magnificent, Glorious, What a gift.
Sent from Heaven to Earth, a curse to lift.

All our sins, evil thoughts and iniquities…
Covered in your blood, we are now set free.

What gift to a Christ Child would I dare to bring,
to my Lord, the Creator over everything?

To you dear Lord I'll give my gifts.
The same ones you've given me, others burdens to lift.

I'll write songs, books and poems to,
For people who know me, I'll work for you.

Preachin, Teachin, and Perfectin the saints,
Using the Bible wherever Satan says, "I **Cain't**!"

This is the gift I'll give to you.
Because one day your Grace made me like New.

Happy Birthday Jesus!

Possessing The Land
For The Glory of God

Joshua 1:11 Pass through the host , and command the people , saying , Prepare you victuals ; for within three days ye shall pass over this Jordan , to go in to possess the land , which the LORD your God giveth you to possess it.

Joshua = salvation, Our spiritual land = Heaven,
3 = solid/real, Jordan = descender,
wealth of another = benefit

The Lord did not hesitate, nor did he stutter, "Have not I commanded thee?
Be strong and of a good courage my people, there's no one to fear here but me!"
Be not afraid, neither be thou dismayed: for the LORD thy God is with you,
He is with thee whithersoever thou goest, and His word alone will stand true!

Then Joshua servant of the Lord, gave all of his officers a command,
Saying, "Surely the Lord is with us now, I know that we'll take this land."
Yes, the Lord spoke to Joshua His servant, and he in turn told each official.
So the duty of obedience once told to the people lies with each individual.

Pass through the host, and command the people, "Saying , Fix something good to eat,
Cause within 3 days we'll cross over this Jordan, and the river will never touch your feet."
And we'll go on to Possess The Land, which the LORD your God has given.

Yes, I know Jericho's walls are 6 feet thick, but they're still no match for heaven!

So my brothers and my sisters we must march on till the final victory is won,
And don't let down, nor even slack your reigns till the residing of the Son.
Yes, that's son like Jesus Christ, cause we're more than a conqueror in him,
And we're soul winners as we let our light shine, because if we hide it we're dim.

Get ahead of your sisters and brothers and encourage everyone in the Faith,
In Christ we will not descend down, but we'll ascend as we rise up from this place.
Make up in your mind, to look for the wealth of another, though that may sound really odd,
Then the Lord will bless you to inherit the land, all just <u>For The Glory Of God!</u>

Reason For The Season

Twas of the Holy Ghost the angel did say,
For the Lord has determined that He'd bless us this way.

And this blessing of which the angel did speak,
Has set men on a wonder their curiosity peaked.

Round Joseph and Mary and their immaculate birth,
Baby Jesus, Emanuel - God with us on earth.

Hearing of Jesus Herod met with his priest.
And determined he'd hood-wink the wise men from the East.

But wise men my friend are not wise without reason,
As a dream from God shows Herod's heart full of treason.

So when they had worshipped the child at his birth,
And presented him gifts found rare in the earth.

They departed for their countries a brand new way,
Pleased to see Herod on yet some other day.

A dream warned Joseph to take Jesus and Mary.
To go live in Egypt and leave in a hurry.

So the prophets foretold of the way he would come.
As Herod slew all the children that were just 2 years young.

So from Egypt land Joseph turned aside to Galilee,
Because it has been written a Nazarene he would be.

Young Jesus had a cousin whose name was John the Baptist,
And this was rather strange for the Father was Zacharias.

John the Baptist prophesied that a Savior would soon come.
But Alas his valiant warning was not heeded by everyone.

So many there be that miss that straight gate,
And follow the serpent to share in his fate.

But Christ I will follow and I'll tell you the reason,
Because Jesus you see is the cause for this season.

The Call Of The Wall

Humpty Dumpty sat on the wall,
Humpty Dumpty had a great fall,
All the kings horses and all the kings men,
Couldn't put Humpty together again.

And so is the challenge when you are Called to the Wall,
Surrender cares to Jesus and you cannot then fall,
Do the Lord's good pleasure whether women, or men,
And the Holy Spirit will help you again and again!

Christ The Redeemer

Christ the redeemer died on the cross.
He suffered all in spite of lost.
He dragged a cross to Calvary.
Bled and died just to set us free.
A tomb as our Savior paid all costs and used his blood to
redeem the lost.

The Season

Now I lay me down to sleep, prayin for God my spirit to keep, but is this spirit worth the time, without His Spirit comforting mine.

They say, tis the season to be jolly, to fill the home with boughs of holly, But is this why we have God's only Son, to spread good cheer to everyone?

They say, tis the season to send cards, to those we care about near and far, But instead of cards why not send prayers, So your loved ones can know you really care.

What's the value of a soul, when Christ doesn't have complete control, And will those carnal make it in when, they are bound by earthly sin?

His yoke is easy and His burden light, and His gifts bring with them Spirit sight, Sight that helps us find our way, when Satan's gloom invades our day.

Now for the harvest, we can give thanks, in spite of the labor that it takes, But who's laboring in the field now white, filled with fresh souls for God's delight.

The harvest is plenty but the laborers are few, these are Christ words and they still ring true, to a world that's dead or dying, while on the flesh it keeps relying.

So just like Peter I must exhort, and convince the believers that they must abort, "Turn from the world you wicked nation, in Christ you'll find your souls salvation."

Now's the season of the Spirit, those with an ear…will surely hear it, Is there room inside your Inn, and when He knocks will you let Him in,

Or is your Bethlehem all-full-up, with no desire to ever sup, with the parakletos, or Comfortor, if you let Him in, he'll be so much more.

Tis the Season of the Spirit, those that have an ear. . . will surely hear it.

Where Have You Been
Why Are You Here, Where Are You Going?

Where Have You Been?
Lost without a rope, Down without a hope?
Drowning in your cares, Lost in a sea of despair?

Why Are You Here?
Here to be shaped, Here to be molded!
Here to be strengthened, Here to be emboldened!

Where Are You Going?
Going to where God sends me,
However God sends me there.
I'm going to the top,
I'm going to outpace my past.
I've made up my mind, I'm going to be with Jesus!

Potter's Clay

Sovereign Jesus, Lord above,
Adonai, we need your Love.
Yeshua HaMashiach is the Great Gods Name.
El Shaddai, Almighty God
Heavenly host spread your fame.
We adore you Jesus,
For your name heals our land.
As an army we raise to serve you.
We are yours to command.
We are dust without you Jesus,
But you use us anyway.
Mend us, mold us,
Great God from glory,
We are the Potter's clay.

12. The Last View

2 Kings 2:15 And when the sons of the prophets which were to view at Jericho saw him, they said, The spirit of Elijah doth rest on Elisha. And they came to meet him, and bowed themselves to the ground before him.

View: sight; vision.

Sometimes we see or hear from someone for the last time. As we each age through the cycle of life it is unavoidable. Sometimes even death comes unexpectantly. We should just expect that none of us are going to live forever. Then live, love and give like it may be our last time.

The passage from 2 Kings 2:15 makes me appreciate this eventuality. The sons of the prophets saw Elijah and Elisha head toward the river Jordan. They knew that Elijah's days were short, and that he would soon be with the Lord. Verse 7 of the passage notes them watching Elijah and Elisha standing on the banks of the Jordan. This was the last time they saw Elijah. At the end they recognized the anointing of Elijah now resting on Elisha.

Sometimes we take our **views** for granted. What could God be showing you by what He has allowed you to see or catch a ***vision*** for? The picture is of my father. It was one taken of him visiting me in my home. It was one of the last taken with several of my brothers and I.

I take this opportunity to be with you as no small feat of God's awesomeness. Running the streets of North Fairmount in Cincinnati as a little lad I had no idea, nor ***view*** that my words would grant me to be put in print.

I close with a few of my favorite works. The first is in memory of my mother. The next poem is an observation concerning our time and endurance here on the planet. Then I share a poem in memory of Dad. Followed by what appears to be the whole motivation for my writing. I pray that you can find a similar motive in unfolding your gifts, purpose and talents. I close this book with, "**The Rapture**". This poem/rap could just as easily have been posted in a section of songs since there is a heavy bass riff that I use to accompany my presentation of it. Walk in your blessings. Keep your eyes open for the best view!

THE WINDS OF CHANGE ARE BLOWING
BUT YOU'VE GOT TO VIEW THE RIGHT STORM

The winds of change are blowing, but before you become alarmed. Know that life's passage always brings a change so remember to view the right storm. Yes, the winds of change have blown hard, on this tight knit family. But GOD alone determines the things that will be.

I for one will be guided not just by the problems in life, but by the lessons I learned from Leotha. A mother, a woman, a wife. She was mother to five men and to two fine young ladies, and she nurtured us all from the time that we were the smallest of babies.

Like the hopes she had for the future, and her insatiable urge to keep giving. This is but one of the many lessons, that I choose to recall from her living. I hold my mother's love dear to me. We'd talk for hours on end, and often we'd talk about Calvary, and how Christ had died for our sins.

But hold fast not this thing we call love, because in clenching great damage is wrought. But cherish its being with each passing moment. An item that cannot be bought.

So dying presents many mysteries that we cannot all readily solve. GOD's hands commands all the answers, and to our hearts brings, true resolve.

The winds of change are now blowing, but before you sound the alarm, know that life's passage always brings a change. So remember to view the right storm.

Though they say that the tempest moves in from the west, don't dread and don't you yet fear. Because the treasures of life may be swept from the east. Yet you know not when it may appear.

We know that storms sometimes leave wreckage, oft attributed to GOD'S wrath. But, if I say wreckage is merely change, you may seek to avoid this path. But if from the rubble a better city is built than before. Then that change yields progress a subtlety of life of which we all claim we want more.

So know that all change is not progress, but all progress requires some change. And when we're caught in a comfort zone we fight a battle that can't be maintained. For change is the order of the universe for all entities except one. Because GOD doesn't change from day to day. A power he shares with none.

See our focus is skewed by society's standards, and things that they like to call "norms". Know that life's passage always brings a change, so remember to view the right storm.

Life is Frail

Life is frail, and fraught with disdain.
Meager a heart when full of pain.

Alone a plan to be made new,
was brought by a man, a savior too!

Now comes to death, eternity.
Not mortal this gift for you and me.

Brought high our hopes, trust and believe.
Yet for today, our hearts still grieve.

Remembering Dad

Just a few words I can say, as I think about my Dad
I remember his care for me, since my days as a lad.

I can recall my days growing up, in what is called the hood.
He would bring the family White Castles, if we all had been good.

Or we may have to sit, at my Dad's TV shop,
While Dad made a run, for a TV that had stopped.

Tinkering and playing with the equipment he had there.
Gave me the confidence to become a young engineer.

These are just random thoughts, so don't think that I'm mad.
They just pop into my head, as I think of my Dad.

Our formative years, were spent in what's called North Fairmount.
Not a whole lot of money, is what that's all about.

There was the house on Beekman Street, but first there was Dempsey.
Dad poured out his wine, so I never saw him get real tipsy.

Reverend Merchant told my Dad, to make my Mom sit down,
But that wasn't happening, after the Holy Ghost came to town.

He put down cigars too, when he finally got good and saved.
He brought his baptism clothes with him, it was the water that he craved!

So after the baptism, a Deacon Dad would be,
I know of the process, because it also happened to me.

Refuge Temple's our home, and our Pastors Bishop Carter.

Years working the ministry, prophesying sons and
prophesying daughters.

Then there's the bell bottoms of the 70's, which were one of the
fads.
And other things I remember, as I reminisce of my Dad.

He drove trucks in the army, is something I recall.
I think that has affected my driving, look a nod from them all.

He and Mom drive up to UD, just to check on my state.
They would bring money and food, and then keep me up real
late.

He was there when I needed him, I cannot complain,
He showed me how to be a man, and to bring honor to my
name.

A home where we served God, and all honored the Lord,
Paid tithes and offerings, and learned to handle our sword.

He gave me an inventive heart, and a creative mind,
An entrepreneur's spirit and compassion for the blind.

I don't mean to waste your time, on some lyrics that are bad.
Yet here are some special contemplations, from being blessed
with a Dad.

Therefore I Write

What is the reason that I write,
What is my main motivation?

To give a voice to those things done right,
To document the resonance of a nation.

To share my joys to share my pains,
To list out what we now all disdain.

These are a few of my celebrations,
That give my solace lubrication.

Yes sir there's more things of which I write,
About the things that bump in the night.

That wake me up and noise that won't cease,
That prevent dreams and black eye peace.

These are some topics for which I write,
Because some come early, at dawns new light.

They speak of things we might never say,
Sometimes sharing when there's truth decay.

Sometimes our right has become our left,
Other times Justice has suffered a theft.

We may catch a train that's come too late,
Or just to speak of those who participate.

These all fill the bill as fodder to jot,
To drop a rhyme about a beat that's hot.

But it's mostly for God, to give Him Voice,
In these exact cases I have no choice.

He says, "Wake up.", then, "Write this down!"
That's the time iPad goes to town.

Its cause I've learned there'll be little rest,
If I don't pour out this gift for which I'm blessed.

Maybe that's all He's tryin ta say,
Just work your gift and you'll be OK.

Therefore I write.

THE RAPTURE

<u>No</u> my brother He's not going to take them all.
Some are going, but others are gonna fall.

Three'll be standing under the shade of a tree.
He'll take two the other will fall to his knees.

He'll beg for mercy but mercy he will not get.
Grace is gone he's in a brand new net.

<u>This</u> nets called trouble, tribulation if you have the time.
Mercy's gone, it's pain you're gonna find.

There'll be buses, gone on a trip to the mall.
But my sister he's not gonna take them all.

He'll take a few but plenty'll be left you know.
All the rest didn't have what it takes to go.

<u>To</u> go to heaven takes more than just be'in kind.
The love of Christ has to consume your mind.

A life of deeds has to be left in your wake.
Cause faith without works only proves you're a fake.

And fakes won't make it so Homey you ain't gettin in.
Neither will liars, or others who live in sin.

<u>A</u> spot or wrinkle, or blemish just won't do.
To please my Jesus you have to be washed like new.

If you're empowered to see sin and turn away.
You'll have the power to make it come Judgment Day.

But watch and pray the spirit's not just to shout.
And once in Christ is not what my faith's all about.

With oil in your vessel each and every night.
Cause only God knows when the time is right.

The Rapture's comin, and Saints it won't be long .
Till you'll be shoutin and singing a brand new song.

A song of Jesus as you're walkin right by his side.
Eternal body allowing you to keep stride.

So turn from sin and from it run away.
And if you're not saved you can come to Christ today.

Conclusion

Come to Jesus Christ today

Have you made a decision to call Jesus your Lord and personal Savior? As the last poem says there is reason to trust that one day He will return. When he does will you be "Rapture" Ready? The Bible tells us that His coming will be... like a thief in the night. However, that is only for those that are not looking for and expecting His return.

If you haven't made a decision to follow Christ and call Him your personal Savior you can do that today. Pray the Sinner's Prayer for salvation. This simple Prayer just provides words that you can state out loud to commit your life to Christ.

Sinner's Prayer:

Dear Lord I, _(repeat your name)_ repent of all of my sins. I have decided today to follow you.

Having prayed the Prayer is superb and it is good a first step. Now let me encourage you to go on in faith in Jesus Christ, observing to do all that He tells us to do in His word, The Holy Bible.

If you prayed the prayer find a good church home, and send me an email. I love to hear about new brothers and sisters coming into The Kingdom of God: dayspringchurch@att.net

Limited Time Offer:

If you just prayed the Sinner's Prayer and have just now come to Christ I'll send you a Rapture √ wristband:

Rapture √implies that you are searching your life regularly against the Bible to ensure that your soul is "Rapture" Ready…Blessings Pastor B.

Dayspring Church of God, Apostolic
2127 Doctors Park Drive
Columbus, IN 47203
(812) 372-9336

About The Author

David C. Bosley was born and raised in Cincinnati, Ohio. He is the founding pastor of Dayspring Church in Columbus, Indiana. He has been pastoring for over 10 years and preaching for 20. He is a published author and the past dean of Calvary Midwest Bible College, and Theological Seminary.

He has attended the University of Dayton and Calvary Midwest Bible College and has degrees in both engineering and theology. He has multiple patent submittals and continues to write poems, patents and Christian books. Pastor Bosley and his lovely wife Charlene have 2 grown children and 2 grandchildren.

Pastor Bosley is available for poetry readings, book signings, speaking and preaching engagements. Contact him through Dayspring Church.

If you would like to request additional copies of this book, or Pastor Bosley's children book, "**Love Came Down At Christmas Time**" please contact us at:

Dayspring Church of God, Apostolic
2127 Doctors Park Drive
Columbus, IN 47203

Website: *http://www.dayspringministries.com*
Email: *dayspringchurch@att.net*

(812) 372-9336

Bibliography:

Book or Magazine, Media **Author**

1. Change or Die, Alan Deutschman
2. Love Came Down At Christmas Time, David C. Bosley, Trafford Press
3. Dr. Martin Luther King, Jr. Statue, Lei Yixin
4. Mandela painted at the DDC, Thierry Ehrmann

5. Mom's 2007 Salary, Salary.com
6. The Look of Love, Burt Bacharach
7. University of Dayton Logo University of Dayton
8. Young Frankenstein Mel Brooks, 20th Century Fox

Index of Poems

List of ***In My Father's Image*** Poems:

1. A Great, Grand, Mother
2. A Heart, A Box, A Key, And A Lock
3. A Mission Still To Fulfill
4. A Mother Is
5. Anniversary Roses
6. Anniversary
7. An Island Or A Nation
8. Apostolic Church
9. A Reason To Hope
10. A Street Of Palms
11. A Taste Of Brotherhood
12. Begin Anew
13. Be Strong Brother Strong_ Remix
14. Black History Month
15. Black Renaissance
16. Bliss
17. Celestial
18. Come See A Man
19. Creative Faith
20. Cross To Bare
21. Dad's Gemstone
22. Dared Dream Of Destiny
23. Daughters of Zelophehad
24. Dayspring Motto
25. Diaspora
26. Faith
27. Faith Hope and Love
28. Friends And Family Day
29. Give God The Best
30. God Inhabits Praise
31. Gospel Extravaganza
32. Grace For Grace
33. Just - Dream
34. Just Stay

35. "Letter From A Birmingham Jail, A Simple Reprise"
36. Let's Go Star
37. Life Is Frail
38. Lord, We Praise You
39. My Gift I Bring
40. My Love
41. My Queen
42. Naturally Never Alone
43. Nelson Mandela: Good Bye Our Hero
44. One Man On Purpose: Rock the Joint
45. Poetic Sampling of Me
46. Porcelain Man or Bonus Man
47. Possessing The Land
48. Potter's Clay
49. Ready For More
50. Reason For The Season
51. Remembering Dad
52. Standing On Holy Ground
53. Stay There
54. The Bitter Cup For Freedom
55. The Calvary Crusader
56. The Call Of The Wall
57. The Dream Alive
58. The Lad From Reelsville
59. The Rapture
60. The Redeemer
61. Therefore I Write
62. The Season
63. The Strength of A Man
64. The Tides That Swell
65. The Winds Of Change Are Blowing
66. The Word Is The Key
67. This Rose Is A Pledge
68. Thy Kingdom Come Today
69. Till The Light Goes Out
70. True Life

Bonus CD Material

Bonus CDs have been inserted in the first 150 books. This is for unique book purchasers at Dayspring Church. If you have a Bonus CD I thank you for being an early adopter.

The following is the list of poems and songs you will hear:

1. **I Want To See Jesus**: *The lyrics and melody are my own. The arrangement and music is by* ***Donel Sallard****.*
2. Stay There
3. A Mother Is
4. A Taste of Brotherhood
5. Come See A Man
6. Daughters of Zelophehad
7. Give God The Best
8. God Inhabits Praise
9. Grace For Grace
10. Just - Dream
11. Nelson Mandela: Good Bye Our Hero
12. A Mission Still To Fulfill
13. The Bitter Cup For Freedom
14. The Dared Dream of Destiny
15. Therefore I Write
16. You Are Precious
17. **In The Beginning**: *The lyrics and melody have been created in collaboration with* ***James Wood, Sr.*** *and his son* ***Jerome Wood****. The arrangement and music is by* ***Donel Sallard****.*
18. The Rapture: *The Bassist is* ***Shannon Luckey***
19. (*Come to Jesus*)

www.ingramcontent.com/pod-product-compliance
Lightning Source LLC
LaVergne TN
LVHW051236080426
835513LV00016B/1609
9780692308653